AMERICAN QUILTS AND
HOW TO MAKE THEM

AMERICAN QUILTS AND HOW TO MAKE THEM

CARTER HOUCK & MYRON MILLER

CHARLES SCRIBNER'S SONS NEW YORK

Text Copyright © 1975 Carter Houck
Photographs Copyright © 1975 Myron Miller

Library of Congress Cataloging in Publication Data
Houck, Carter.
 American quilts and how to make them.
 Includes index.
 1. Quilting. 2. Coverlets, American. I. Miller,
Myron, 1918– joint author. II. Title.
TT835.H63 746.4'6 75-5541
ISBN 0-684-14111-6 (cloth)
ISBN 0-684-16272-5 (paper)

3 5 7 9 11 13 15 17 19 M/C 20 18 16 14 12 10 8 6 4 2
1 3 5 7 9 11 13 15 17 19 M/P 20 18 16 14 12 10 8 6 4 2

Printed in the United States of America

CONTENTS

AMERICAN QUILTS AND
HOW TO MAKE THEM

INTRODUCTION

Some people like to look at quilts and some people like to make them. Some others like to look at them and dream that some day they are going to make them. We planned this book with the intention that it might appeal to all of those people. In this way the person who thinks about making a quilt but never gets around to it will not have just a book of unused patterns but a book of pictures of really beautiful quilts to enjoy and look at and leave on the coffee table.

We also felt that the quilts are a bit like very fragile spring flowers in that they look best in their natural setting and fade some if they are just seen hanging flat. All the little furnishings as well as the beds and other large pieces of furniture make them seem more like what they were, a part of everyday life, and less like a self-conscious piece of art. So, all of the examples in this book were photographed in places similar to the ones from which they might have come. Few historical houses are lucky enough to have the furnishings that originally belonged in them but they have authentic and lovely examples of the era or eras in which the house was occupied by its family.

3

Some of the designs we chose are well known but are especially good examples of those designs such as the Oak Leaf Cluster, p. 168, and the Sunburst, p. 159. Others are wonderfully imaginative and show great ability to use a standard design as a departure point for creativity. Two quite opposite ones that fall into this category are the Whig Rose, p. 190, and the Tulip and Wandering Foot, p. 123. There are others which display real artistic originality like the Stratford Beauty or the Thistle Crib Quilt.

We looked at a lot of quilts in many historical houses, museums and restorations, and rarely saw two which were more than somewhat alike. If the pattern had once been the same, the use of color, the size of the pieces, the way the squares were joined or the choice of border made the variation so great that it was hard to say, "We saw this pattern last week." What was even more astonishing as we contemplated it was that there were hundreds, probably thousands of other houses that we never even saw which also had quilts different from the ones we did see. We saw enormous and varied collections in the larger museums and in brochures of those museums but didn't use them because the settings of the smaller places fitted our format better. Our final feelings were of frustration that we would never see all or even half the beautiful quilts in existence and of delight at the great variety of the human imagination.

These are presented to you to enjoy just as they are or to use to spur your own imagination. There are some patterns and some suggestions but very few rules for you to go by. If you are a rank beginner, you will find some designs that are easy enough for you if you take your time and read the directions for cutting and stitching. If you are an accomplished quilter, there are a number of challenging designs in their entirety and some ideas that you might get from such complex pieces as the album quilts. Whatever you use the book for, we hope that you enjoy it as much as we enjoyed making it.

QUILTS
AND HOW THEY GREW

Now that American Folk Art has come into its own, quilts have become recognized as America's special contribution to the world of art. The women who pieced and stitched the lovely bed covers of the eighteenth and nineteenth centuries could hardly have envisioned them vying for wall space in the museums that house Titians and Rembrandts. It may have seemed that the men who cut down forests and killed Indians were making a far bigger contribution to the future of the country than were the groups of ladies happily occupied around the quilting frame. Fortunately tastes and thinking have changed in time to rescue many quilts from attics and oblivion so that now there is hardly a museum or historical restoration in the country without at least a nice small collection of quilts.

The fundamental idea of quilting came to America with the first settlers. It had been introduced into Europe, as were many textile arts, by the men returning from the Crusades. What they brought back were padded garments made of two layers of cloth stitched together with a layer of some warmer fabric between. The comfort and practicality of such clothing worn next to the skin was quite obvious in an era of metal armor and unheated dwellings.

BEDROOM IN THE VANCE BIRTHPLACE   Anyone interested in American textiles will find the Vance Birthplace restoration a real treasure trove. The numerous quilts, mostly early to mid-nineteenth century, and the overshot coverlets are always on display in a setting which completely suits them. The album quilt on the bed, though made up of very simple designs, was planned by someone with a good artistic eye. The quilt on the trundle is exquisitely stitched. We were told that the pieced design is called Cake Plate, though it bears a strong resemblance to the Basket designs. It is also a close cousin to the Single Saw-Tooth on p. 79. The quilt folded on the blanket chest is a good example of early one-patch designs, being made up of rectangular blocks in two colors.

Ladies in the northern countries such as Holland and England soon applied the padding and stitching technique to their own clothing. At first the stitching was done in simple diagonal lines or squares but by the fourteenth century women were designing intricate patterns for their vests and petticoats. Bed covers were quilted for extra warmth and then valances and bed hangings or furnishings were quilted decoratively to match. The end result was so elaborate and beautiful that sets of bed furnishings were often mentioned in wills. Certain patterns grew up in specific areas and became easily recognizable as having originated in a certain county or town. Names and dates were often worked in, a habit which has made it easy to place the exact time and place of many quilts.

When the first European settlers came to New England, they certainly brought a few quilted coverlets and petticoats with them and they soon had need of more. They could import very little material so for the most part they worked on rough homespuns of their own wool and linen. The same types of all-over stitched designs were used that had been used for several centuries. At first the quilts were mostly dark-colored wools or linsey-woolsey; later more elegant ones were made of white linen or cotton with fine white-work stitching in carefully planned designs such as the ones on p. 8 and 9.

This fine linsey-woolsey quilt, brown on one side and glazed blue on the other, was woven and quilted by Mrs. Mary Doty of Morris County, New Jersey, who was born in 1759. It can now be seen in the Ford Mansion, Washington's Head-quarters, in Morristown.

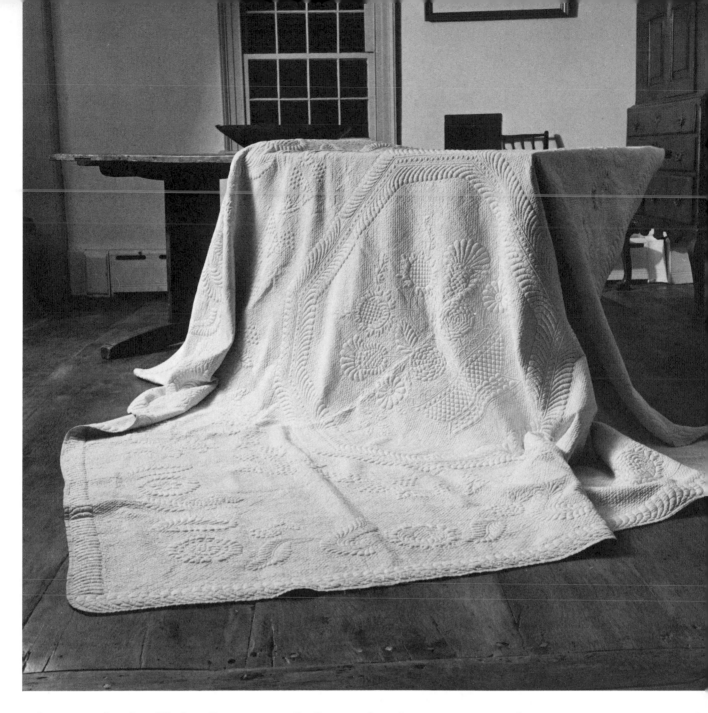

A fine example of padded quilting or raised white-work is this 1816 piece in the collection of the Hoyt-Barnum House in Stamford, Conn. It was made by Lucy Foot of Colchester, Conn. who used many of the traditional designs of the time in her own artistic arrangement.

As fabrics wore out, old garments were cut up and sewn together in patches and, when a big enough piece had been made of patches, it was quilted or simply tied through at intervals. Some were made entirely of squares or rectangles but others were created from all sorts of shapes intricately fitted together into what is known as a Crazy Quilt. As patched or pieced quilts grew in popularity, the all-over stitched designs of white work were still made through the nineteenth century. White work was also combined with the other techniques and fine designs of flowers and feathers and fruits were stitched into the more colorful quilts that had their heyday between the Revolution and the Civil War. (See p. 67)

Other patch shapes which developed early were the triangle and the hexagon. Very soon it became apparent to the more artistic eye that if the colors were arranged according to a system, quite intricate designs could be made. The Mosaic or Grandmother's Flower Garden pattern, still popular today, appears in a million variations but always using the one hexagon shape, often several thousand in a completed quilt!

The designs became more elaborate, though always geometric, as the population moved west. They became known as pieced or piecework quilts and in some places as string quilts. This last name came from the long narrow strips or strings of fabric left over when a garment was cut from a length of fabric. The shapes that made up the whole designs were often quite tiny and dozens of them could be cut from a string that was too small to be of use for anything else.

The simplest way to arrive at a new pattern diagram was to fold a square of paper, so that one square folded could become four squares and then perhaps eight triangles. Patterns quickly moved from one-patch to two-patch, four-patch and nine-patch according to the way the square was folded. Inside the four or nine patches might be any number of smaller shapes, still geometrically formed.

Though these designs were not representational but abstract, they began to acquire names. The names varied with the locale and often with the whim of the maker. As many as six names are often used for one design and another six for variations of that design. One name often means two different designs to two different quilters. This leaves room for endless battling between authorities but most people have come to accept the fact that when someone says they have a Robbing Peter to Pay Paul, they may

It takes a keen eye and a good sense of color and shading to produce such harmonious variations in the simple Grandmother's Flower Garden pattern. These and a number of others in this same one-patch design were made by one woman for various members of her family and are seen here in her daughter's 18th century house.

produce any one of several designs which in turn can be called by any one of several other names!

Out of frugality and necessity, the great American piecework quilt, our true folk art, was born with imagination and a sense of fun. At the same time in parts of the country where life was not quite so hard, appliquéd quilts made of delicate imported fabrics grew in favor. In the late eighteenth century families who could afford to buy French toiles made quilts of fine linen or cotton with cut-outs from the printed fabric appliquéd in lovely, rambling, all-over designs. Cotton prints from India were used, sometimes in cut-out form and sometimes left whole and quilted to a filling and backing.

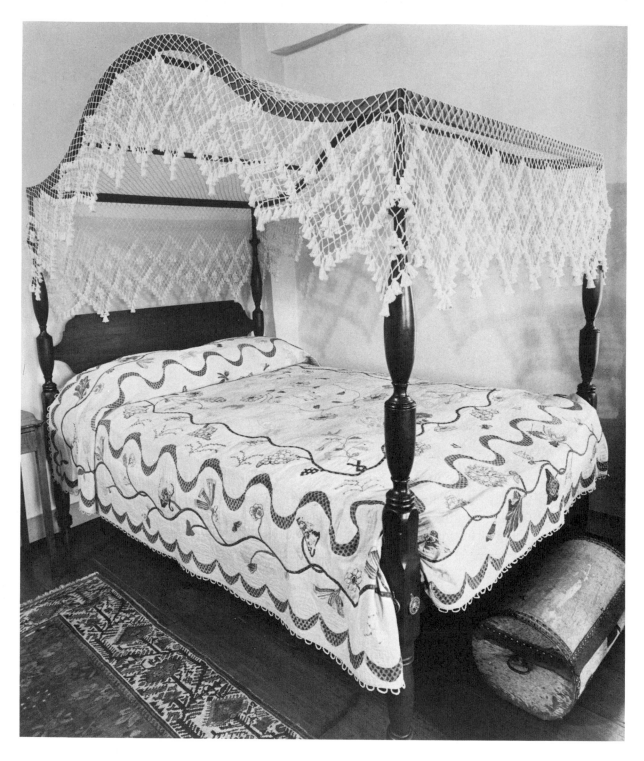

The Bush-Holley House in Greenwich, Conn. proudly displays this early (1810) quilt covered with cut-outs from printed chintz worked together in a design of vines made of bias strips of printed fabric. Both the scallop and the double scallop borders are made from one simple crescent shaped pattern.

The plain white linen or cotton fabrics used for backing and background were generally woven in America, often by the same women who quilted on them. Solid colors were dyed at home, sometimes with vegetable dyes and sometimes with commercial dyes. With the advent of roller printing and copperplate printing, colorful patterns of domestic chintzes and calicoes became available in local stores.

Both appliqué and piecework flourished and grew in the early nineteenth century. Piecework patterns were largely limited to straight lines for easy assembly, except for a few designs such as The Reel, p. 61 or Orange Peel, p. 149. Appliqué knew no such limitations and so opened up enormous possibilities for pictorial themes. Quilts began to blossom with gardens, historical scenes, and happy records of family life. Whereas one might be limited to simple stars and sunbursts in piecework, every flower that grows could be stitched in appliqué. Favorite subjects were roses, cockscombs, thistles and iris (known in Southern gardens as "flag"). Wreaths of roses and vines laden with grapes and huge baskets of flowers appeared. Although the same themes were used over and over, each person planned and drew and stitched them in her own way.

One of the more interesting outgrowths of this highly individualized art was a series of variations called Album, Autograph, Freedom, or Friendship quilts. Some elaborate Album quilts were made as presentation pieces for a local minister or doctor. Freedom quilts were for young men when they reached their twenty-first birthday and many Friendship quilts were made as engagement or wedding presents for young women. Each square was usually made by a different person. In some cases there are a number of designs, often a wonderful potpourri of piecework, appliqué and cut-out appliqué, as in the Friendship quilt on p. 88. Some of the squares in this quilt might have been made of scrapbag pieces but a coordinated effort produced several from one fabric, including the chintz cut-outs.

A part of the Friendship or Freedom quilt idea is for each person's name, date and even a verse to be written in. This might be done only in indelible ink but was frequently embroidered with the tiniest cross stitch or stem stitch. For this reason the designs with large white center spaces were also very popular for Friendship quilts (see p. 116).

In some Album quilts the fabric must have been purchased by one person and divided up among the ladies who were to work on it. This, plus all the squares being designed by one very artistic person, added up to a very professional and formal-looking presentation piece (see p. 133). In the years between 1840 and the Civil War the most elaborate work was done in the form of padded appliqué like Italian Trapunto and white work which echoed the designs of the appliquéd blocks. All of these marvelous variations appear in the Album quilts of that period.

There are all sorts of stories about the system of parties that grew up around the planning and making of Album or Friendship quilts. When one member designed all of the patterns to be used, there had to be a party so that each lady could draw for the one she was to work on. As the designs often ran from a simple wreath to an elaborate basket of flowers, the outcome was of some concern to the participants, who all wanted the quilt to look as uniformly magnificent as possible. If each designed her own square, then there had to be a party or get-together to plan for the best arrangement for them. Sometimes one person joined the squares or "set" them but that too could be a joint effort. At the end there had to be a "quilting bee" to stretch the quilt on a frame and finish it with thousands of fine stitches, often in intricate patterns.

These communally-made quilts are among the best preserved examples of American quilting in museums and collections today because they were presentation pieces and, like loving cups, were admired rather than used. The simpler Friendship ones seem to have undergone more family wear and tear than the more elaborate Album quilts, which indicates something about the way people treated these different types of quilts. The young bride undoubtedly knew her friends meant her quilt to be used and enjoyed, whereas the minister was under some constraint to keep his work of art (presented by a formidable group of women) in its original mint condition.

Sadly for quiltmaking in America, Victorianism, the Reconstruction Period, and a general decadence in art and taste soon followed. After about 1870 houses and the furnishings in them became over-elaborate to the point of opulent confusion. Quilt patterns went the same way! Silk and velvet with bits of ribbon and lace were the new materials from which this once-simple art was now wrought. The four-sided Log Cabin pattern grew in size and splendor and the Crazy Quilt became burdened with layers of silk embroidery depicting saccharine children and smug pussycats along with quite graceful flowers, fans, and spider webs. Historic and sentimental themes vied for first place, often a large square in the center of the quilt. Most of these confections were of a smaller size than their forerunners, often a throw for sofa or chaise, living room show piece rather than bedroom necessity. In their own way the late nineteenth century silk throw quilts were like the last glorious but rather ridiculous fling of a beautiful woman just before she settles down amid recollections and echoes of her life.

Fortunately the echoes did not totally die away. Though no new patterns came into being, the old ones were copied and pieced in cabins in the mountain areas of the East and across the country in farm houses on into the twentieth century. There are many women still, especially in Pennsylvania and the Appalachian regions, who can claim to be at least fourth generation quilters and who have saved examples of work from that far back in their families. Patterns have been exchanged and scraps collected and a few groups continue to get together for "quilting bees."

The renaissance of needlework now sweeping the country is just in time to pick up the thread of knowledge and expertise which winds its way down from the first settlers. There are still enough examples of the fine stitching done before the takeover of the sewing machine, the patterns are still intact in museums and private collections, and a whole new generation of quilters is gathering for lessons and for "quilting bees."

EQUIPMENT FOR SUCCESSFUL QUILTING

Fortunately no one has been able to invent a lot of expensive electric equipment for quilting. There aren't even many tempting but useless gadgets on the market to lure the quilter and make her spend money. The largest item on her list is a quilting frame and that can be built at home quite simply.

Long before you need the frame, you need a few other simple tools. In planning a design of your own, you should have a good ruler, triangle, and a French curve. Firm paper, stencil paper, or thin plastic should be used for making the pattern pieces so that they won't wear out if you have to draw around them over and over. The large flat pieces of plastic from the sides of bottles are firm and yet thin enough to cut with scissors. You will also need a medium hard pencil and a chalk pencil.

You will need very sharp scissors to cut the many pieces of fabric required for most quilts. To keep the pieces segregated by shape, color or design use plastic bags. As you cut, you can put all the red corner triangles in one bag and the blue center squares in another, etc., keeping count as you do. This system not only keeps things sorted out but also keeps them clean.

Short needles and fine pins are required for the type of precise joining that is done in either appliqué or piecework. If you've never used a thimble before, invest in a comfortable and preferably pretty one. Put it on and wear it; after a while you will start using it. The alternative is to wear a callous on the end of your middle finger! When you get to the quilting part, stitching back and forth through all the layers, you may need a protector for a finger on the other hand, though a piece of tape, strategically placed, will do the same thing.

Work surfaces are important. If you are tracing patterns instead of drawing around them, make a simple light box. A sheet of glass set up on two piles of books with a small light bulb on an extension cord laid under it is adequate. Just be sure that the glass is fairly thick and that you don't lean your whole weight on it. For drawing around the stiff cut-out patterns, use a table at a comfortable height or a lap board which fits across your chair arms. There are two useful eyesavers for any type of needlework. The tensor lamps, especially those which can be swivelled around in so many positions, keep the light right where you need it. Most needlework stores now carry a magnifying glass that hangs around your neck and props against your chest so that your hands can go right under it when you are doing especially fine stitching.

If you intend to do your own quilting and not just piece or appliqué the tops, frames become very important. Few of us have large studio rooms in which we can leave a full-sized quilt set up on a frame indefinitely. Even though a quilt on a frame is a decorative object, families are apt to take exception to watching TV across one for ten years. Other than having a very large living room or a workroom of your own, there are various alternatives.

One early description of what was needed as a frame for quilting was "four stout sticks," which very nearly describes this frame in the Conyngham-Hacker House attic in Germantown. The holes bored in the 1″ x 3″ pieces enable the user to peg it onto the ingenious legs for changes in size. These same "four stout sticks" can be bolted together and rested on the backs of four straight chairs when in use, enabling you to set the whole frame up against a wall out of your family's way. The bolted frame can also be suspended by ropes through rings or pulleys in the ceiling. In this way it can be lowered and rested on your lap or on chair backs and later pulled up out of the way.

The sturdy frame in Belle Grove would be simple to build today but does require space in which to set it up and leave it, though it can be dismantled for storage when not in use. The crossed legs are of 2″ x 4″s and the rollers are 2″ x 2″s with the ends whittled to fit the holes, as shown here. The legs are fitted securely together where they cross with a half lap joint like a well made picnic table. The crude ratchet and pawl can be cut out of metal with fairly primitive tools or you can have them made in a metal shop. For another view of it, see p. 20.

Frames of this type, four sticks pegged or bolted together, are as practical now as they were over a hundred years ago when this one was made. It is now displayed with an unfinished quilt properly lashed to it in the attic of the Conyngham Hacker House in the Germantown Restoration in Philadelphia.

A roller type of quilt frame is very practical because it can be made narrower than the bolted or pegged variety and one person can reach all the way across the exposed part of the quilt. The metal rachet and pawl seen here are a simple but highly efficient means of keeping the rollers tight and locked in place.

The full view of this roller frame at Belle Grove in Middletown, Va. shows how neatly a quilt can be rolled so that the finished part and the part not yet started are out of the way. One or several people can work conveniently at such a frame and it is attractive and not too large to leave up in the living room.

There are many frames available in stores or mail order catalogues if you are not inclined to go into woodworking yourself. A sort of in-between solution is a blue print for building your own which is available from Stearns and Foster, who make quilt batting and other quilters' needs. (See pp. 196–197)

The most portable and easiest to store of all frames are the large round "lap frames" like the antique one pictured here. The new ones are about the same size, over 20″ across, and are made to hold any thickness of fabric. Some people seem to be able to quilt neatly with no frame at all, though this is risky if you are not thoroughly experienced. Both of these last methods require that you baste very well. For more information on that look at the chapter on construction, p. 42.

A modern young lady may find it more convenient to work on this antique lap frame than on one of the larger stationary types. The charming Sunbonnet Girl quilt is in the process of being made as a keepsake with all the fabrics from one girl's wardrobe from age one to twenty-one. Modern versions of the frame are available.

WHAT GOES INTO A QUILT

Years ago, when the first quilts were made in America, many were created from start to finish, from raw fiber to fabric and filler and every careful stitch, by one woman. By the beginning of the nineteenth century it was easier to purchase not only imported fabrics but calicoes and chintzes printed in America. Fabrics were fine but dyes varied a great deal so that many have faded and some have eaten through the fabric.

The earlier quilts were of wool or linsey-woolsey and sometimes filled with wool. Cotton was easier to handle as a filler and was preferred by most quilters. By the middle of the nineteenth century ready-made quilt batting or filler appeared on the market.

The final touch on any quilt was the binding, which was usually made of a bias piece of one of the fabrics in the quilt top. Some mid-nineteenth century quilts were finished with a strong woven cotton twill tape that was extremely durable but not particularly attractive.

By looking back at the collections of antique quilts, the quiltmaker of today can benefit from all the accumulated knowledge of the centuries in choosing the ingredients for her work of art. Today fabrics are marked

23

for fiber content, color-fastness and shrinkage. The same is true of batting and binding. Shop carefully in the store and select carefully from your scrapbag, always taking into consideration that your time and talent deserve the best in material.

There are still finely-woven 100 percent cotton fabrics on the market, although they are harder to find than the cotton blends or synthetic mixtures. Unfortunately, only time will tell whether the latter will wear as well over the period of a hundred years or so as the best pure cotton, but if they are of a good grade and meet your needs in color and print, it seems safe enough to use them. If you are a purist, search in catalogues and country stores for the 100 percent cottons, some of which have been made recently largely to meet the demands of quilters.

Besides checking your fabric choice for fiber content, check it for color-fastness and shrinkage. If it has any residual shrinkage, and most washable fabrics do, rinse the whole piece in warm water and hang it flat to dry before you cut. When you are dealing with scrapbag pieces of uncertain origin, it is wise not only to pre-shrink them but to lay the darker colored ones on a white towel when they are wet to see whether the color might bleed. If it does, it would be very unwise to incorporate it with the light colors and white.

Crazy quilts are about the only designs suitable to fabrics other than cotton, though some simple one-patch designs (see Irish Chain, p. 143) can be interesting and serviceable in hard-finish wools. Crazy Quilts, such as the late nineteenth century one in the color section, can be made from all the velvets, velveteens, silks, fine woolens, and ribbons in your scrapbag. Very few of the synthetics masquerading as silk will be effective, but old ties are a fine source of perfect silk pieces. If you are reusing old garments and ties, be sure to have them cleaned first. The coin-operated cleaners are a satisfactory and inexpensive way of doing this.

Sometimes it is wise to back the pieces of fabric. If you are using scrapbag pieces and, for sentimental reasons, feel that you must include very lightweight dimities, organdies and the like, you should back the piece as soon as it is cut with a piece of fine batiste or muslin, also pre-shrunk. Some of the very large pieces in the floral appliqué designs are easier to handle and will stretch less on the bias if they are backed. Most of the old silk and velvet quilts that are still in good condition have not split because the pieces were backed. It is as true of silk today as it was in the nineteenth century that it has a shorter life span than cotton, linen or wool.

The backing or reverse of your quilt is important too, so choose the fabric for it carefully. Again you will have to decide between the harder-to-find 100 percent cotton and the cotton blends. It is still possible to get pure cotton muslin or percale sheets and sometimes wide sheeting by the yard. There is a slight difference in the way that the pure cotton and the blends handle and, when dealing with a large piece, most people prefer the pure cotton. Some of the nineteenth century quilts had marvelous printed backs (see the red and green on p. 113) which, with their intricate stitching, were almost as pretty as the fronts. If you want to make that kind, you should use the same print as one used in the quilt top, which you will have to seam together in strips to get the full width needed.

Filling or batting comes in a nice variety of sizes, from crib to extra large, and in both cotton and polyester. For the look of the authentic, rather flat, early American patchwork, cotton batts are preferable. If you want a higher loft, as you might in more modern designs and in the silk and velvet quilts, the polyester will produce the proper effect.

Even thread makes a difference! First you must decide on the proper color or colors. Much piecework can be done entirely with white thread but appliqué must have the correct shade for each piece that is to be sewn down, as even the best blind stitching shows just a bit. Usually the quilting is done all in one color to correspond with the backing. Again cotton thread seems somewhat easier to work with, sliding more smoothly and knotting less than the synthetics.

The final step is binding, which should be chosen and sewn with great care as it seems to be the first thing to wear out on many antique quilts. The most attractive thing you can use is one of the fabrics from the quilt top, cut on the bias. If the fabric is fairly lightweight, there is a better way to use it, called French double bias, described on p. 46. The ½″ or ¾″ cotton twill tape makes a virtually indestructible, but less attractive, binding. Commercial bias binding, sold in packages, is rarely of as good quality as the fabric in the quilt top, so beware!

A last thought on what goes into your quilt; be generous with yourself. By laying the pattern pieces on a measured space and multiplying by the number of them that you will need to cut in each color, you can approximate the amount of fabric needed. It is a bit like the recipe for cooking rhubarb, though: "Put in all the sugar it will hold and then add a cup." Always add a little extra to the yardage after you are sure you've calculated enough and allow an extra yard of the color from which you will cut bias binding.

Besides the fabrics, batts, thread, and binding there are two other essential ingredients to any fine quilt, love and patience. How much of each of these went into many of the antique quilts is easily told by the beautiful and lasting results.

DESIGNING
AND PATTERN MAKING

Designing quilts is very much like designing clothes in some ways. It is always hard to say whether the choice of fabric or the choice of line comes first, or whether they combine in your mind over a period of time, each one suggesting the other as the idea grows. You may have a bag of pieces which you get out and look at and lay out in certain rough designs until the day you see a quilt that seems to be much the way you want your quilt to be. Or you may invent a design based on ones you've seen but planned to fit a specific bed or room or color combination. Then you will probably go out to buy the fabric that the design calls for.

You will have to decide on the pieced or appliquéd design for the squares and on the colors to be used and which one will be predominant. The way that the squares are joined can be of great importance and the borders can change the entire look of the quilt. Except in cases like the Grapeleaf Reel, p. 54, and the Floral Fantasy, p. 162, where the border is an integral part of the design, borders can be chosen almost at random to suit the fancy of the quilter. The joining or "setting" of the squares is a bit more of a problem. There are some designs which cannot be put together in any other way than "edge-to-edge" without destroying the intricately planned optical illusion. Look at Melon Patch, p. 113, and Robbing Peter to Pay Paul, p. 170, for two fine examples of "edge-to-edge" setting.

Both borders and "sets" can be handled artistically in piecework, in white work, or in plain bands of color. The width and proportion in relation to the rest of the quilt is what really determines the perfection of the final artistic effect. Cross-bar sets can be white and nicely quilted, as in Puss in the Corner, p. 116, or they can have a piecework design of their own as in Indian Trails, p. 151. The elaborate white work border on the Giant Tulip, p. 103, sets off the bold design of the four blocks better than any colored or appliquéd border could.

With all these things in mind, choose your design and your borders and "sets" and do some arithmetic to see that you can make it all come out to fit the bed, preferably as magnificently as in the case of the Star of Bethlehem, p. 126! Remember that you can make many of the designs for squares larger or smaller than the patterns that we give you. If you are good at graphing designs to reduce or enlarge them, do it that way and then cut out all the pattern pieces in tissue paper and lay them together to make sure that they fit. Another method is to have them blown up or reduced professionally. This can be done photostatically or with an instrument called a pantograph, which is quite simple to operate and might even be worth buying if you do many needlework designs.

When you have all the pieces of your patterns drawn or traced or enlarged perfectly, transfer them to your stiff paper or thin plastic so that you can draw around them as many times as you need to. In all of your work with the patterns it is useful to have good rulers and drawing equipment as described in the chapter on equipment so that your lines are smooth and curves neat and proportions accurate. It is hard enough to deal with small pieces of fabric when they are cut perfectly, but inaccurately cut pieces are sure to make you give up quilting almost before you start!

Be sure that the pencil or chalk pencil that you use to trace around the pattern pieces is *not indelible* as it is apt to show through light colors even though you do all your marking carefully on the wrong side. Hold the pattern piece firmly in place with one hand as you draw around it so that the fabric won't pull or move with the pencil. If the piece is large and the fabric has a tendency to wriggle, you might try working on a soft surface like a cork board and using push pins to hold the pattern and fabric in place. Trace a number of pieces, leaving at least ½" spaces between, and then cut them out, leaving ¼" seams all around. You will very soon get so accustomed to the seam width that you can cut it accurately almost without looking.

One other thing that you should think about when you are placing the pattern on the fabric is the grain line. There are bound to be bias edges on some pieces in any pattern except a design made of squares only. Sometimes seaming two bias edges together can be troublesome and the results slightly ripply. With this in mind, you might work out systems of cutting that will enable you to put straight grain against bias as often as is possible. This will help to stabilize the square and keep everything flat. When you've figured out the best possible grain lines for each piece, draw them on the pattern with a ruler so that you will be aware of them as you cut. Even though bias edges will fall together sometimes, you will have less trouble in the geometric designs if you have *true bias* and *true straight*, so avoid careless cutting. It is possible to detect the grain line in any woven fabric, even scraps, especially if you look at the wrong side.

The other patterns that you will be using are the ones for quilting or white work designs. The straight line designs can best be drawn lightly on the surface of the fabric with a sharp, fairly hard pencil and a ruler. On large areas of white work where you have quite intricate designs, you have more of a problem. You can make a template of firm paper or thin plastic, as for the piecework and appliqué designs, and draw around each one lightly. In some cases, such as leaves with veins in them, you can fill in the inside lines free-hand without too much error.

There is an old system of using perforated paper patterns and powdered chalk for accurate marking of very intricate designs. You can draw the pattern on paper of about typewriter bond weight and then perforate the lines with a sewing machine. Use a large, no. 18 needle, unthreaded, in the machine and set the stitch at 6-to-the-inch. Very slowly stitch along each line. After you have laid the pattern on the fabric and poured the powdered chalk on it, you will need to rub the chalk a bit to make it work through the perforations in the paper. Both white and colored chalks are available.

If you have drawn your white work pattern on medium-weight paper, you can transfer it to most white or pastel fabrics by using a light box, described in the Equipment chapter. Lay the pattern on the glass and the fabric on top of it, turn the light on, and lightly trace the pattern onto the fabric with a hard pencil or chalk pencil.

There are now some more modern marking methods that you might check into. Dressmaker's carbon in some brands is guaranteed washable so that, in combination with a tracing wheel, it should be an easy way to transfer white work designs. However, skepticism forces us to suggest that you use it on a scrap of your white fabric first and see how much effort is required to remove the lines. There are also nylon-tipped pens containing washable ink, generally sold at needlework shops for use on fabric, which may be easier to use than hard pencils for tracing around cutting patterns; the line seems too heavy for tracing white work.

Once you've made all the big decisions about design and fabric and color and have assembled your equipment and made your patterns, you're ready to start stitching a quilt. The first part is to piece the top, then you can decide whether you are good enough and dedicated enough to do the quilting or whether you will have to give in to reality and have a semi-professional quilting group do it for you.

ABOUT THE PATTERNS IN THIS BOOK

There are 57 patterns in this book which can be used to make the exact quilts shown in the pictures, or as a stepping stone to designing one's own quilts. In the case of the Pennsylvania Album Quilt, p. 88, one design might be used for an entire quilt. In many cases borders might be exchanged and certainly the "sets" might be varied. Some people feel that there are very limiting rules in quilt making, such as always using only pieced borders with pieced designs. We feel that it is the very latitude allowed the quilt-maker which has developed such a varied art form, so we give you the patterns with as few rules as possible.

The pieces are given in full size to be traced and used as shown in the reduced piecing diagrams. In a few cases the pictures are so bold (see Thistle Crib Quilt, p. 100) that a piecing diagram does not seem necessary. When cutting pieces, remember that *seams must be added*. The same is true for the required bias strips, whether the width given states that it is a finished width or not, that is what is meant and seams must be added to the amount suggested.

When the pattern pieces were diagrammed, they were cut in sufficient numbers in paper to lay together one whole design for the purpose of checking the measurements and angles. It is wise to do this again when you make your stiff patterns so that you are sure of the number of pieces needed for each square and that no error has crept in during the tracing. If you don't want to spend the time doing this, at least make up one whole square in fabric before cutting the entire quilt.

There are some quilts pictured for which no patterns are given for a variety of reasons. It is obvious that most album quilts are very personal and must be personally designed. We hope that the ones shown will provide incentive to a new generation of quilters. Some of the one-patch designs are shown simply to illustrate an era, as is also the case with the silk and velvet Victorian types. There are several quilts shown as examples of one woman's inventiveness, in some cases using standard shapes in a new way as in Silk Game Board, p. 57, and in others using shapes in a completely free and artistic form such as Fruits and Florals, p. 53. Again, they should serve as inspiration rather than pattern.

COLOR CHART FOR PIECING DIAGRAMS

Color	Pattern	Color	Pattern
Red		Yellow	
Green		Hot Pink	
Blue		Pink	
Pale Blue		Teal Blue	
Brown		Tan	

SEW IT
ALL TOGETHER

You've looked at the pictures, you've assembled the equipment and the materials. You've got it all together so there's nothing left to do but make a quilt. Briefly, this is how it goes: trace and cut all the pieces and separate them into the plastic bags. Piece or appliqué them, usually into small squares, join them together to make the top, baste the top, the batting and the backing together and quilt it, bind the edges; you have a quilt! There may be a few things you should know and think about first.

Be sure your fabric is all pre-shrunk and pressed. Sort the colors, if it is a scrapbag quilt, and decide which shapes and how many to cut from each color. Work on a flat surface and draw the shapes on the back of the fabric as described in the chapter on designing and pattern making.

PIECEWORK

If you are making a piecework quilt, figure out the best sequence for joining the pieces for each square. Try to avoid having too many corners to work around, as a matter of fact, try to avoid having any corners to work around! For instance, if you were making T-blocks on p. 178, you would assemble it like this, making nine sections (it is a nine-patch design) and then joining those so that you have three strips and then joining those.

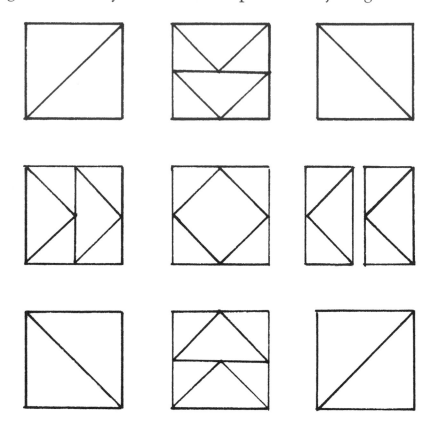

Sometimes it is unavoidable to have corners to sew around, so learn the best way of dealing with them and practice. One way is to sew one seam right to the corner, then fasten off the thread and sew up to the corner from the other end. Clip the corner after fastening off the last stitching, unless the fabric ravels easily, in which case it is better to press the seam all one way instead of clipping so that you can press the seam open flat.

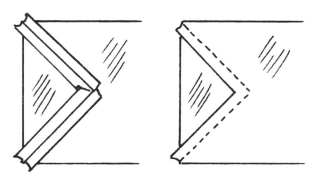

Seam clipped   *Seam pressed one way*

The other alternative for sharp corners is to stay-stitch the inverted corner so that you can sew the seam neatly around it. At this point we may cause an argument with the purists because the best way to stay-stitch is on the sewing machine with about 12-stitches-to-the-inch.

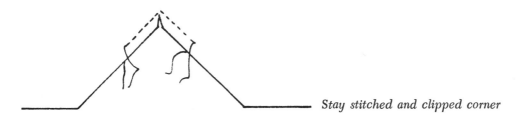

Stay stitched and clipped corner

A corner is sometimes formed by the joining of two pieces into which a third piece will be set. In that case you can leave a ready-made clip at the corner when you first join the two pieces. Sew only to the marked seam line when you make the first seam and fasten the thread securely. Sew the third piece in up to that same point along each side and fasten off; don't try to cross the first seam line as you turn the corner. When you are through and start to press the seams, you may want to clip out a bit of the corner material to avoid bulk.

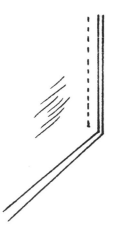

First step of three-piece corner

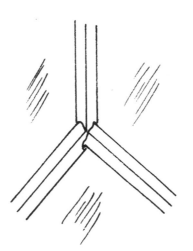

Finished three-piece corner

Curves are even trickier than corners, which is why only accomplished quilters should try piecing Caesar's Crown, p. 178. The best beginner quilt with curves is Orange Peel, p. 149, and even it may be quite a challenge. Stay-stitching on the concave curve is almost a necessity and again we are in favor of doing it on the sewing machine (with the tension set so that the fabric doesn't pucker). Stitch on the marked line, a little more toward the raw edge than toward the center of the piece, because you have to leave room to get the seam-stitching very close to the stay-stitching, but on the marked line. The stay-stitching will be concealed in the seam so, if you do use the machine, it will never show. After stay-stitching and before joining the pieces, clip around the curve at intervals of ¼" to ½" straight down toward the stay-stitching. Then you can pin the concave to the convex piece smoothly, pinning the ends and the center first and then working between. When you stitch the seam, always keep the clipped side up toward you.

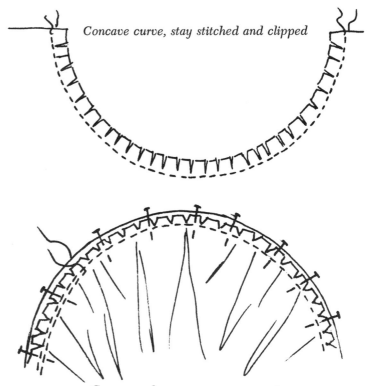

Concave curve, stay stitched and clipped

Convex and concave curves joined

One word of warning about piecing; it is done with the simplest running stitch, but even that requires some skill. If the stitches are not even or if the thread is pulled too tight, the fabric will pucker and not lie smooth. You may be sure that the situation will not improve; if your piecing starts out to look rough and uneven, it will fit together less well as you add more pieces. That is not to say that a little gentle pressing won't improve a newly pieced top, but it will not cover the glaring errors! For another way of piecing that helps to keep everything flat, see the section on backing and stiffening, p. 40.

APPLIQUÉ

Appliqué is usually done on squares, octagons, or diamonds of quite manageable size, though The Cutpaper Cockscomb, p. 96, was definitely appliquéd after the white background was seamed together, and The Reel, p. 61, had the stars put on the corners after the squares were joined. Borders also have to be appliquéd in rather large pieces. The point of this is to say that a 12″ to 30″ square is a lot easier to cope with than a large piece, so, if you're about to do your first appliquéd quilt, pick a design that you can keep under control. There are many good floral appliqués with easy outlines and some of the wreaths and leaves are not too difficult. You can make up your own cut-paper designs or you can borrow ideas from the album quilts. Appliqué does not have to be as exact as piecework and leaves more room for individuality.

Curved pieces, and that means most appliqué pieces except the bias strips for stems, should be stay-stitched for easier handling. Again, the machine does the best job on this if you just have your tension right and your stitch fairly small. The same rules apply as in stay-stitching for piecework; the stitching can be even farther into the seam allowance, still following the marked line, so that it can be completely turned under. Clip all the corners, almost to the stitching and, where the curve is very convex, cut out small narrow notches to keep lumps from forming in the fabric when it is turned under.

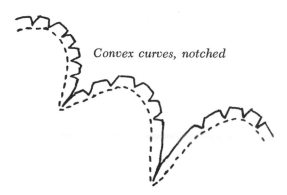

Convex curves, notched

You may press the edges under along the stay-stitch line or you may finger press them or baste them as best suits you and your way of working. In the very loose designs with lots of long stems and leaves, you will certainly find it easier if you draw the plan on a piece of paper and then trace it onto each white square, so that all the appliqué pieces will be put down in the very same arrangement. In The Reel and related designs where we suggest piecing the center part, it is necessary to keep all the pieces very exact as they are appliquéd onto the square. Look at Oak Leaf Cluster on p. 168 and you will see how much the symmetry enhances the design.

Working on a flat surface, lay each appliqué piece in place on its square and pin or baste it in place. If you have basted the edges under or even pressed them so that they will stay in place, you may pin all around with the pins crosswise to the edge of the design. Pin strategic points first and then pin between. The other way is to pin the pieces down in a few places and then baste them about ⅜″ from the stay-stitch line. As you stitch each piece in place, you can turn the ¼″ seam allowance under without interfering with the line of basting. Use your needle to push the corners in nicely and to make sure that all the stay-stitching is hidden underneath.

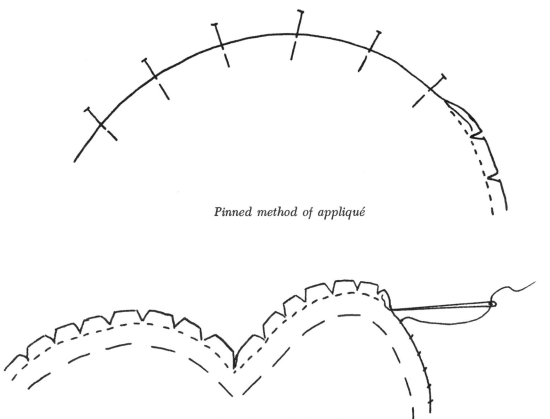

Pinned method of appliqué

Basted method of appliqué

There are several stitches which can be used for appliqué. The neatest and most traditional stitch for fine needlework is the blind stitch. Start underneath and bring the needle up through the basic fabric and the tiniest edge of the appliqué. Put the needle back into the base fabric just over the edge, only a thread or two from where it came up, and run it underneath for less than ¼″. Bring it up through the edge of the appliqué again and repeat the process. If the thread matches the appliqué perfectly and your stitches are very fine, the work will be almost invisible.

Blind stitch

Buttonhole stitches, again very fine and even, are another sign of excellent workmanship. Use an embroidery thread, two or three strands of 6-strand, or a fine pearl cotton, for the best effect. Make the stitches firm, always pulling the edge up tightly against the edge of the appliqué piece, and be sure to keep the spacing even. The diagram shows the way the stitch works, but don't feel bound to do it down or toward you if it feels more comfortable another way, just so long as you throw the thread before every stitch and come up through the loop. The stitches on The Stratford Beauty, p. 137, are not even ⅛″ deep and are the same distance apart, which is just right for a delicate, smooth finish.

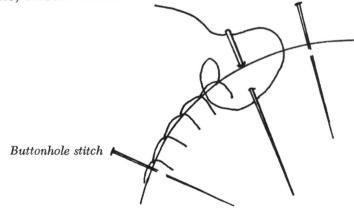

Buttonhole stitch

A running stitch can be used, and was in some very crude quilts, but other than being a good way to let a child start out, there's not much merit in it for appliqué. If it is used, it should be very even and close to the edge.

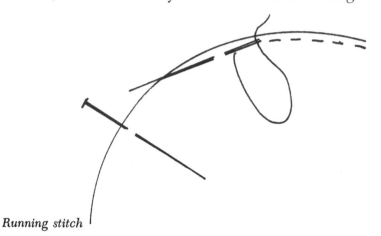

Running stitch

When the ladies of the late nineteenth century made all those silk and velvet Crazy Quilts, they used every imaginable stitch to outline their blocks, but it seems unnecessary to go into that here. It would take an entire book on embroidery to explore all the herringbones and feather stitches, single, double, and triple, parading in profusion across the silk and velvet throws. Suffice it to say that not only were the stitches a challenge to the imagination, but the threads used were luxurious and varied—silks of all colors and silk ombres shading through an entire range of tones and colors were especially popular.

One more trick of needlework can be used in appliqué to show the skill and imagination of the quilter. The designs can be padded, as in the grapes on The Baltimore Album, p. 133, or the Kentucky Sunburst, p. 194. This is a simple matter of pushing a bit of batting under the design when it has been stitched down about two-thirds of the way around. Use a fine knitting needle for this and distribute the stuffing so that it is even, then finish stitching around the piece.

BACKING AND STIFFENING

If you do need to use backing or interfacing under some of your fabrics to make them handle in the same way as the heavier ones, a fine white muslin, batiste, or underlining fabric (pre-shrunk) can be pinned to the back before the stay-stitching is done. It will then be held in place by the stay-stitching and the two layers will be handled as one. If you don't mind taking advantage of more modern methods, there is a very thin non-woven interfacing product on the market which can be ironed on the back of each piece. Cut it exactly by the pattern, without seam allowance, and iron it onto the back of the fabric piece. This also gives you a firm edge to work against and may make stay-stitching unnecessary. Both of these methods will work on either piecework or appliqué quilts.

An old tried and true method of handling wiggly little pieces with lots of bias edges in piecework is to use a paper backing on each piece. Again, in many cases the thin iron-on interfacing will usually achieve the same thing, the greatest difference being that the paper comes off after it has served its purpose and the interfacing stays in, so the finished result will feel slightly different. If you are working on a Star of Bethlehem, p. 126 or a Silk Gameboard, p. 57 then you will certainly need to stabilize all those little pieces in one of these ways. The interfacing may have one other advantage on silk in that it will keep it from splitting when it ages.

The way to handle the paper backing is to cut each piece of paper, letter-paper weight, by the pattern, without seam allowance. Lay it on the back of the fabric piece and fold and baste the ¼″ seam allowance neatly over, folding in the corners and sewing through the fabric and the paper. Do several pieces like this and start by laying two of them right sides together and whipping or slip stitching them together. Be sure to use very tiny stitches and catch only through one layer of the fabric, right on the folded edge. When you have joined all the pieces of the point of a star or the flower on Grandmother's Flower Garden, p. 11, take out the basting, retrieve the paper pieces for re-use, and press gently on the wrong side of your work. You may find that it is worth the extra trouble, because, in the long run, you're apt to have to rip and re-do a great deal of your work in an effort to keep such designs flat if you just seam them together. The iron-on interfacing may be a good compromise for those of us who become impatient with too much basting!

Paper backing method

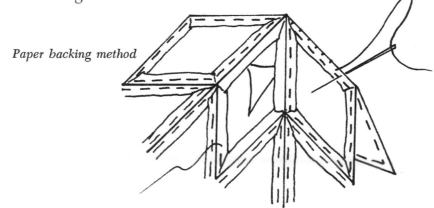

ASSEMBLING THE TOP

Assembling the quilt, either with or without "sets"—the strips or squares of fabric joining the patterned squares—should be no problem at all, provided that all the squares were made carefully and the dimensions are accurate. Quilts like the Grapeleaf Reel, p. 55, would be especially hard to piece together if there were errors in arranging the appliqué on each square. Most people who are making the Robbing Peter to Pay Paul types start putting the squares together after making only a few so that they can test the accuracy and the effect.

When the top is all joined together and the border, if there is to be one, added on, you may feel that it looks a little tired from being worked on so long. It won't hurt to wash it gently in a mild cold water detergent or soap in warm water. Don't machine wash it at this stage because it will ravel on all the raw edges which are exposed. Wash it by hand in the tub and rinse it several times to be sure that all the dingy water is out and won't run down to one edge when the quilt is hung to dry. Hang it over a straight rod, not on a line that sags down. If it drips dry, you should only have to press it lightly.

BATTING AND BACKING AND QUILTING

Seam and press the fabric for the backing, unless you are using a sheet which requires no seaming. The back should be a bit larger than the top, about 4″ each way, because the top can usually be stretched tightly and made larger than it looks when it is first all joined together. Lay the backing down, the batting on top of it, and the quilt top on top of that. Work on the floor with no furniture in the way, if possible. Use weights, tacks and any members of your family that you can assemble to help in pulling the whole thing tight and even. Pin everything together and then baste, across the quilt both ways and diagonally both ways. At this point you will see why a crib quilt is such a good first project!

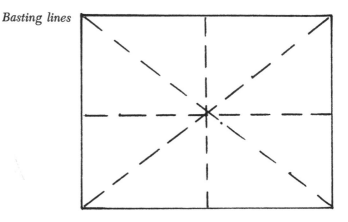

Basting lines

The rollers of the frame should have some old soft cloth (cotton summer blankets are great) secured tightly around them so that the end of the quilt can be pinned to that. As you can see in the Germantown frame, pp. 19 & 81, the sides can be stretched by attaching them to a piece of webbing, which is then tacked to the side bars. The roller frame at Belle Grove, p. 45, is narrow enough so that this is not necessary. However you go about it, stretch your fabric as tightly as possible. If you are planning to quilt without a frame or in a lap frame, you should do a lot more rows of basting while the quilt is still flat. The frameless method makes it very hard to get the tension of the quilting right, so that it holds the quilt firmly together without puckering.

Depending on the thickness of your quilt and how adept you are with a needle, you may be able to take running stitches, several at a time, using your other hand to help guide the needle (this is where that finger protector that we spoke of in the Equipment chapter will come in). Most people find it necessary to keep one hand above and one below the frame and push the needle back and forth between them.

Some of the simpler forms of quilting, such as echoing lines retaining the shape of the appliqué, should not require any marking. The elaborate white work should be marked as described in the chapter on patterns.

The ultimate in quilting is the padded or Trapunto type where some or all of the design is stuffed and has a three-dimensional look. Many people say that it is necessary to slit the backing slightly to get the padding in. If you use a fairly loosely woven cotton fabric for the backing, you can get one type of padding in with a yarn needle. Select a soft fluffy synthetic knitting yarn, thread it into a metal yarn or tapestry needle and run it in the area to be padded. Run as many strands in as needed to raise the design, then trim the ends off close to the fabric. Give the fabric a little tug and the ends will disappear inside.

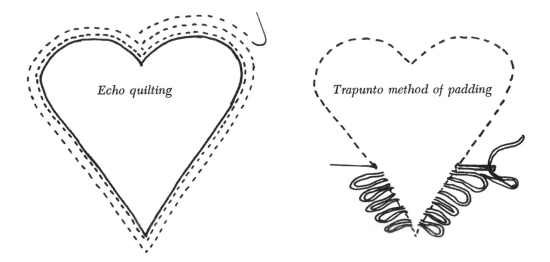

Echo quilting   *Trapunto method of padding*

BINDING

The best binding is cut in true bias strips from one of the fabrics of the quilt top. Use a yardstick and pencil or chalk pencil for absolute accuracy. The binding should be four times the desired finished width, 1½″ for a finished ⅜″ is the usual. Sew it, right sides together, on the edge of the quilt, which has been trimmed evenly after quilting, taking a scant ⅜″ seam on both binding and quilt. Turn it over the edge and turn the raw edge under a scant ⅜″ and whip it along the seam line on the back.

Binding sewn right sides together on edge

Binding turned to wrong side and blind stitched

This is the way an all white quilt looks on the frame while it is being quilted. The design is traced on in a very pale blue. The quilting frame at Belle Grove is used by the curator who also keeps the overshot looms busy.

If the fabric is fairly thin or you think the quilt will receive hard wear, use a French double bias. Cut it six times wider than the desired finished width. Fold it down the center and seam both raw edges to the quilt edge. Now, when you turn it over the edge to the back side, you will have a folded edge ready to blind stitch to the seam line on the back.

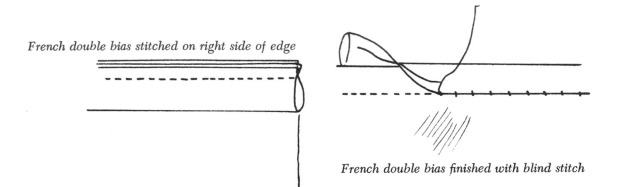

French double bias stitched on right side of edge

French double bias finished with blind stitch

We could go on forever with suggestions for fine finishes for your quilts but we hope that the readers who are only beginning will find sufficient material here to work by. We hope that those who wish to copy the masterpiece quilts in this book, such as the Floral Fantasy, p. 162, will be skilled enough to figure out the extra intricacies of the scalloped border and triple set octagon for themselves. We hope that if you never make a quilt at all, you will enjoy looking at the ones our ancestors made!

CARE AND RESTORATION OF QUILTS

Care of a new quilt that you've made yourself does not present the problems that are inherent in the care of old quilts. In a new one you can be sure of the washability of fabrics and the color-fastness of dye. In an old one you must test, carefully on the corners, to see whether colors will run or bleed. In an old quilt there is also the problem of any undue strain causing the fabric to rip. A new quilt can even be washed in a machine on a delicate cycle and partially fluff-dried in the drier. An old quilt should be washed by hand and this requires a rather large sink or the bathtub.

When you hand wash a quilt, one big problem is the rinsing, as every bit of dirty water must be removed. Any that is left will run down into one end when the quilt is hung to dry and cause a gray area at that edge. Try to get someone to help you and rinse in clear water at least four or five times. If you can spread the quilt between two lines, it may dry more evenly. Use mild soap or detergent and only very mild bleach, if any. If there are iron-rust spots or other difficult spots, you may use a stain remover, purchased in drug stores in a tube, called Gartsides. It is quite safe on white areas, but test a drop of it on colors, especially browns. Another time-tested home remedy for stains is lemon juice and salt and then a good sunning before rinsing the mixture off. Again, test the colors.

Obviously the silk and velvet quilts will have to be dry-cleaned rather than washed. Find the kind of cleaner who specializes in wedding gowns and ball gowns and try not to worry about the cost! It may be advisable to have a cotton quilt cleaned if it seems too fragile for the wear and tear of washing. However, it will never come out as white and fresh as with soap and water.

Storing is another problem if you are a collector. If you have a guest room where the children and the cats and dogs do not romp, a prize quilt is well off in its native habitat, spread on a bed. Ideally one should hang quilts flat, but if the collection gets very large, that becomes impractical. If you hang them against a wall as decoration, it is wise to have a clamp made for the top, using two strips of wood that can be screwed together to hold the quilt edge smoothly between. If you incorporate a large sheet of heavy-duty clear plastic to hang over the surface of the quilt, this further protects it from dirt and hands. Whenever a quilt is on display, make sure that it is not in a sunny spot.

If quilts are to be stored away, they may be hung over large stole hangers (available in any closet shop) thus making a minimum number of folds. If they are to be folded away on shelves or in drawers, there is a dark blue tissue paper which can be folded in with them for protection from light and fumes. Any tissue paper is better than none but a local museum might be able to give you advice on types made especially for the storing of textiles. This is a relatively new field so that there are better things appearing as the museum need becomes greater. Remember that if there is any wool content, moth protection should be used. The same chemicals can also be useful against silverfish, crickets and other insects which will damage cotton. Beware of mice; they have made away with large sections of otherwise beautiful antique quilts! Take your quilts out once or twice a year, air them, refold them on different lines and repack them.

If you have a really large collection, it might be worthwhile to set aside one section of a room in which you can have large wooden rollers installed in a rack against a wall. These can be quite simple, long poles dropped into slanted cuts in two boards fastened onto the wall. The quilts can then be rolled wrong side out and unrolled when you wish to display them. In this way they are not worn by folding and are not exposed to the sun.

Restoration is quite difficult, but necessary if a collection is to be kept from falling apart. Edges often have to be rebound, or if you wish, you might just baste a protective bias strip around the edges in the way that the hems of evening gowns are kept clean in good stores. If the fabric is strong but the stitching has ripped, it is easy to blind-stitch pieces back together. The real problem is when or whether to replace worn pieces. If they do not appear to be continuing to tear, it may be safest to leave them alone. If you can get a really good match on the fabric that was used, you might remove an entire piece and replace it. Some examples of this, though well-meant, are very unattractive.

Museums are using sheer fabrics over the worn spots for protection against further wear. The one which comes most highly recommended is crepeline, which seems only available in large quantities direct from France. It is an extremely sheer silk and the museums use mostly an off-white or light brown which blends well with the old colors. Look around for a good grade of silk organza (not as sheer but usable), polyester chiffon, or wedding veil tulle. The latter can be dipped in tea which will darken it and soften it. Turn the edges of the sheer fabric under and slip baste it over the area which is disintegrating.

Remember that a collection is to enjoy so protect it as best you can, but try to keep it available for viewing. No textiles will last forever but you can help them to have a long and happy life.

OUR HISTORICAL HOUSES

Many of us cringe when we see old and beautiful buildings being torn down to make way for progress. As a matter of fact we feel that the bulldozer and the wrecker's ball take us backward and destroy the best of what our country has built. The people who have felt strongly enough to band together and save houses and villages and to see that they are rebuilt and maintained have done it for all the rest of us. The museums and museum villages and historical houses, which are run by dedicated people, are there for everyone to see and enjoy, a living part of our past.

In this book are the ones which gave us their time and help so that we were able to photograph the quilts in their proper setting. There is not one on this list where curators didn't speak of things that would be completed when they got the money or things that could be done if they had enough help. In quite a few volunteer help is appreciated and depended on for many interesting jobs. In all of them we got the feeling that these are our houses, full of warmth and beauty, and that their keeping their doors open to hundreds of school children and amateur and professional historians depends on what all of us can do for them.

49

The quilts that we show in this book we often found tucked away in drawers because there are as yet no facilities for textile displays. One museum has over sixty quilts in trunks in the attic, awaiting a time when better use can be made of them. So, don't expect to see the quilts where we show them but do go to the houses and villages and take your friends and your children. There are always fascinating things on display, furniture and textiles and china, as well as the little tools and instruments of daily life. There are frequently demonstrations of spinning and weaving, of cooking and preserving, and a dozen other crafts. Several museums are running series of classes in all of these skills and quite a few have large special exhibits of quilts or folk art or weaving at least once a year. If there is an historical house in your community, get in touch and stay in touch for a real experience with the past of your country.

KNAPP'S TAVERN (*PUTNAM COTTAGE*)

On the Boston Post Road in Greenwich, Connecticut, stands one of the most interesting seventeenth century houses on view in New England. It was built by Timothy Knapp and used by his son, Israel, as a tavern for travelers between Boston and New York. One such traveler was the Revolutionary General, Israel Putnam, who was in the area checking on his Connecticut militia. It was during his stay there that he made his famous ride down the steep bluff nearby to Stamford for reinforcements when the British attacked Greenwich.

One unique feature of this house is its fish scale shingling, which gives the exterior an interesting rough-hewn texture. When the decision was made by the D.A.R. to restore the house completely to its seventeenth century appearance, the marvelous central stone fireplaces were uncovered. Anyone interested in the restoration of old houses will find the work of peeling off two and a half centuries of alterations an extremely interesting feature of a visit to Knapp's Tavern.

See color section for Turning Wheels, a fine silk and velvet Victorian throw shown on the piano at Knapp's Tavern.

HOYT-BARNUM FARMHOUSE

In 1641 twenty-eight families settled the town of Stamford. They purchased the land from the New Haven Colony (who had purchased it from the Indians) for the sum of thirty-three pounds! In 1668 Joshua Hoyt acquired a "house lot" which he later willed to his son, Samuel, who built the house just before the end of the seventeenth century. Samuel was a blacksmith and added "Smith" to his name to distinguish himself from several other Samuel Hoyts. The basement room in the house may have been his shop and is now furnished with the type of tools he would have used, plus many other interesting pieces of equipment from the seventeenth and eighteenth centuries.

The Barnum family and their heirs, the Ferris family, later purchased and lived in the farmhouse as the city grew close around them. The last owner, before its purchase by the Stamford Historical Society in 1942, was Agnes Bemish. By that time the house and its small lot stood in downtown Stamford. It is now an oasis of grass and shrubs and nostalgia in an area of high rises and shopping centers and heavily trafficked streets. The Stamford Historical Society has done an outstanding job of restoration and a continuing job of education for which it has won awards and national recognition.

PADDED TULIP   Adeline Scofield Briggs of Fairfield County, Connecticut, was born in 1834 and lived until 1924, during which time she made several quilts. This one is of her own design and was obviously used and loved until it came to rest, in the box which she painted for it, in the Stamford Historical Society's Hoyt Farm House. The ingenuity, craftsmanship, and true artistic talent of America's needlewomen is displayed so refreshingly in works like this where no commercial pattern was used and imaginative touches such as the box were added with a great sense of fun. For Mrs. Briggs's tulip pattern see p. 52.

PADDED TULIP   *Each design is appliquéd diagonally onto an 18" white square. All sections of the flower are heavily padded. The large stems are bias pieces, 17" x 1½", the small branches are bias pieces, 6" x ⅝".*

The quilting is mainly around each design and in simple white work motifs throughout.

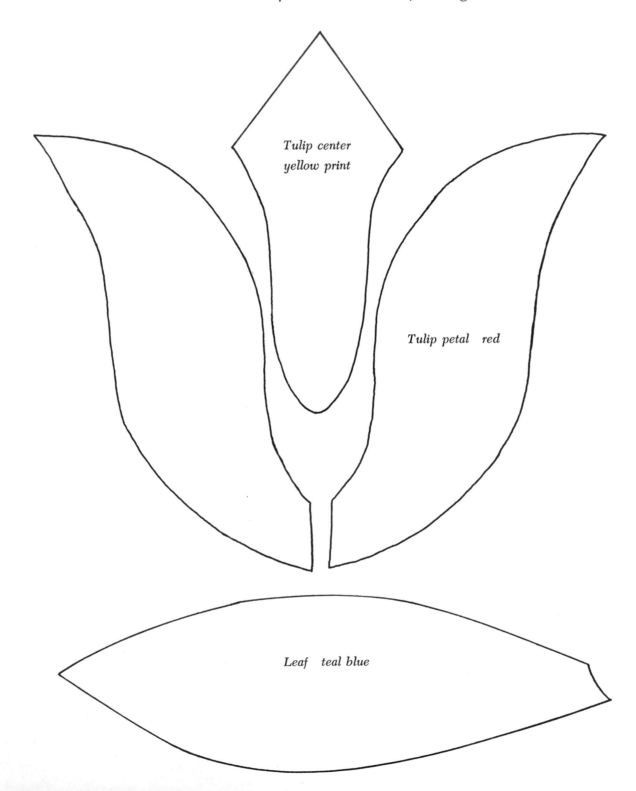

Tulip center yellow print

Tulip petal   red

Leaf   teal blue

BATES-SCOFIELD HOMESTEAD

The New England saltbox is perfectly represented in Darien, Connecticut, by the Bates-Scofield Homestead, rescued and maintained by the Darien Historical Society. It now stands on the edge of a large, modern shopping center which threatened its existence in the 1960's until the Historical Society took it over and had it moved. The original six rooms have been carefully restored to the time of its building, early eighteenth century. A large addition has been put onto the back to make room for the historical society's needs and for a gallery which houses changing exhibits.

The Congregational Church has the first records of this house which it used for a meeting place in 1730 when it was occupied by Jonathan Bates. It later passed into the Scofield family, a name which is found in records of most of the towns of Fairfield County, Connecticut. Although the house was occupied up until the time of its removal and modern conveniences had been put in by its owners, the basic shape and style remained unharmed.

FRUITS AND FLORALS There have always been artists who "did their own thing" and a young girl named Eunice Lockwood, who made this elaborate quilt in 1845, was one of them. She was only seventeen years old at the time she designed and worked this masterpiece. It falls into no particular category though we might call it a one-woman album quilt. Some of the motifs are padded, the stitching is near-perfect and the white work fine. One wonders whether she went on to even greater heights or whether she stopped after she made this one elegant quilt. It is now a crowning part of the collection in the Darien Historical Society, where fine quilt exhibits are sometimes given.

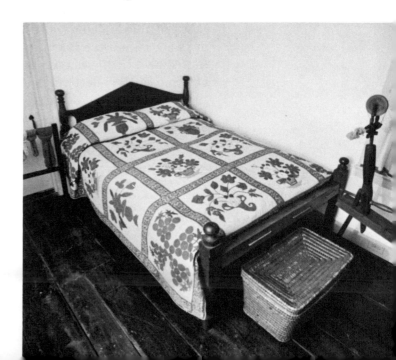

BUSH-HOLLEY HOUSE

We tend to think of New England saltbox houses as being small and frugal. Not so the grand Bush-Holley House, which was even fairly large when it was built in the late seventeenth century but which grew into almost a mansion as the Bush family expanded. They were not the builders; no one is quite sure who was; but they purchased the house and land in 1738. In 1763 David Bush built a tide mill opposite the house. The mill burned in 1899 but the pond and dam are still there, almost under the Connecticut Thruway.

Edward Holley purchased the house and mill in 1882 and ran it as the Holley Inn, a refuge from the heat of New York City. It was frequented largely by artists and writers, many now famous names. Emma Holley, Edward's daughter, married one of these artists, Elmer Livingston MacRae, and continued to live there until the Greenwich Historical Society purchased the house in 1957 to rescue it from the road builders. They have furnished it in a charming mixture of periods, just as it was when it was lived in continuously by the two families. The gardens also have been beautifully planted and restored.

GRAPELEAF REEL   It seems that a dedicated quilt hunter could spend a lifetime tracking down variations on certain themes. Anything related to The Reel or Oak Leaf Cluster would rank high on the list of infinite possibilities and this mid-nineteenth century one should hold its own as one of the most beautiful. The edge-to-edge arrangement of the large squares creates an intricate double pattern unlike the Oak Leaf Cluster (p. 168) in which every square is neatly framed and stands alone. The leaves have been widened to match the grape vines in the border so that it can no longer be called an Oak Leaf Cluster. Because of this and the sense of motion given by the edge-to-edge placement of the squares and the Reel design in the center, we've renamed it Grapeleaf Reel. It is shown in the master bedroom of the Bush-Holley House where it is part of a fine small collection. Patterns are on pp. 55 & 56.

GRAPELEAF REEL *The squares are large, 17″ square, which makes this an exceptionally good design for large beds and a fairly easy design to make. It can be entirely appliquéd in one color on white or the center (pieces #1, #2 and #3) can be pieced and that part plus the leaves appliquéd, piece #2 will not be used.*

The border is 13″ wide. The bias strip used for the vine is finished about ⅝″. The grapes are effective if padded slightly.

The entire quilt is finished with simple diamond quilting. Either red or white binding can be used.

¼ size piecing diagram

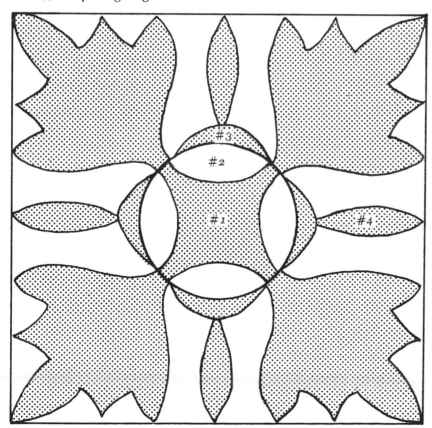

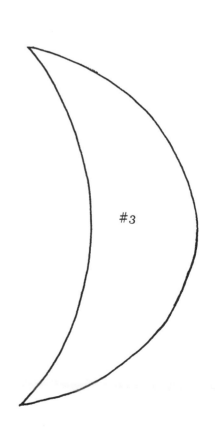

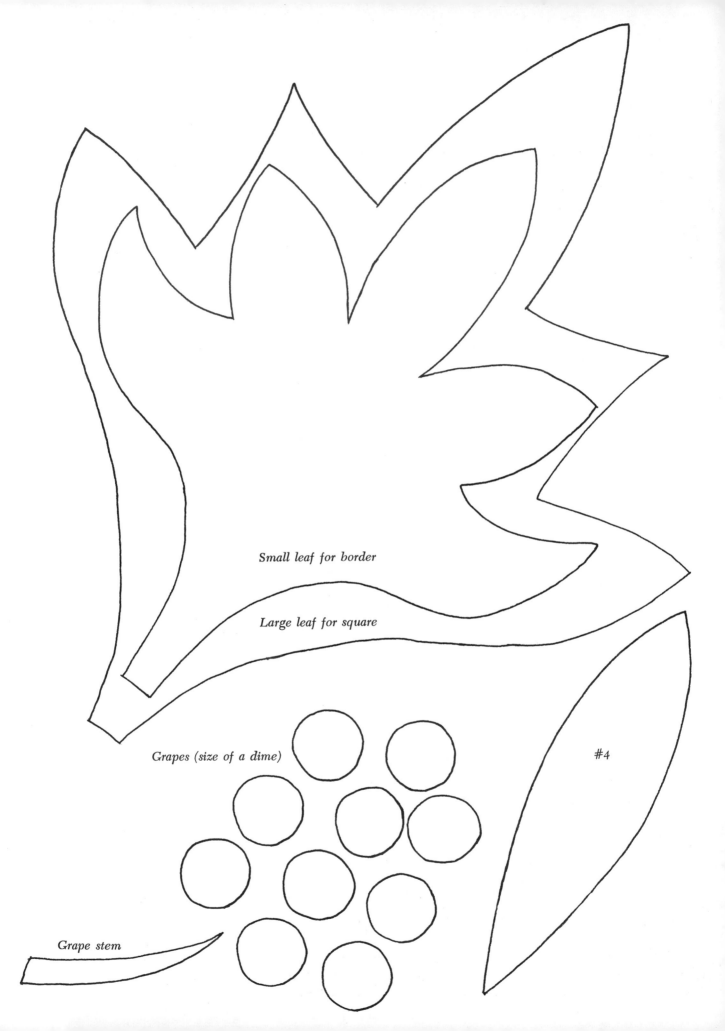

Small leaf for border

Large leaf for square

Grapes (size of a dime)

#4

Grape stem

FORMAL ALBUM QUILT *See page 133*

ALBUM AND FAMILY QUILTS   These quilts represent almost the height of quilting, especially in the Middle Atlantic states, appearing and fluorishing from about 1840 until after the Civil War. They are very individual in feeling though certain designs such as the flower baskets, wreaths, and cut-paper patterns appear in many forms in most of them. They may have been designed and made by one, two or many women. They may represent certain parts of a family's life or they may have been masterpieces created for presentation. Here are four quite different ones, shown not for copying but as inspiration for twentieth-century quiltmakers.

The most formal Album quilt shown here is the red and green one with its careful borders and padded appliqué and intricate white work "sets." Two of the blocks are signed, presumably by sisters, Mary and Elizabeth McComas. Though it is over a hundred years old, it is in near perfect condition, making us believe that it was a gift to a doctor or minister who reserved it for show when guests came to stay. It is shown in the Enoch Pratt House at the Maryland Historical Society in Baltimore, exactly the sort of grand town house setting that it deserves.

The quilt shown hanging on the front porch of Sully Plantation, though on loan there from a private collection, seems in keeping with the practical frame

TYPICAL MID-19TH CENTURY ALBUM QUILT *See page 167*

FAMILY ALBUM QUILT *See pages 64–65*

house. It has many of the same basic designs that are used in the more formal Baltimore Album but it is put together without any elaborate planning other than to center the Mariner's Compass and surround it with four baskets of flowers. It is quite worn as though it had been used and washed often and the signatures that it once had are almost washed away. The workmanship in it varies enough to make it possible that it was made by several people. Two dates are visible, 1862 and 1863.

Family Album quilts are the most fun of all. You can spend hours looking at them and contemplating what the family was like and trying to read all sorts of meaning into the symbols. Was that house like the one they lived in, did the children draw those delightful figures in the lower left, why was a teacup important, and whose hand prints are those up near the house? Most of all, why does it have two dates thirteen years apart? It is shown on the quilting frame in the Lake Tysen House at Richmond-town Restoration, where it is part of a large collection.

COCKSCOMB *See page 118*

WHIG ROSE *See page 190*

DRUNKARD'S PATH
See page 176

T-BLOCKS *See page 178*

SIMPLE STAR *See page 77*

OAK LEAF CLUSTER *See page 168*

SAWTOOTH *See page 79*

PADDED TULIP *See page 51*

GRAPELEAF REEL   *See page 54*

FRUITS AND FLORALS *See page 53*

MELON PATCH *See page 113*

INDIAN TRAILS *See page 151*

CAESAR'S CROWN *See page 178*

PATRIOT'S QUILT   *See page 128*

WREATH AND HEARTS   *See page 145*

SILK GAME BOARD *See page 57*

FLYING GEESE *See page 69*

FLORAL FANTASY *See page 162*

SILK AND VELVET VICTORIAN   When the Victorian era was at its height in the late nineteenth century, quiltmakers used all of the simple early designs in the most elaborate fabrics and embellished them with embroidery. Here we have Tumbling Blocks, a standard one-patch design, exhibited in the Howell House in Germantown, glowing in the colors that only silk can have. The Crazy Quilt (next page) incorporates not only silk and velvet but commemorative ribbons and masses of silk embroidery. It seems absolutely in keeping with the parquet floor in the museum at Richmondtown, both perfect representations of an era of overabundance in design! The Turning Wheel design of this Victorian masterpiece at Putnam Cottage (next page) is an eight-sided variation on Log Cabin, one of the earliest designs. It can also be set in another way, creating the familiar Pineapple pattern. It is, of course, from a much later period than the building of Putnam Cottage but that house was lived in by many succeeding generations and was altered in the nineteenth century to conform to the ideas of design of that time. (It has been restored to its original style.) Therefore both the quilt and the eighteenth-century piano on which it is draped are properly displayed in this pre-Revolutionary house.

TUMBLING BLOCKS

TURNING WHEELS

CRAZY QUILT

RICHMONDTOWN RESTORATION

A lovely hilly area in the middle of Staten Island was settled before 1700 and by that year was known as Cocclestown. By the middle of the century it was a real village with a courthouse and jail, churches, shops, taverns, and a number of houses. After the Revolution the name was changed to Richmondtown and growth continued. It was the county seat until Staten Island became part of New York City in 1898.

Recent years have not dealt kindly with Staten Island. Its rolling hills have become too attractive to developers and, in many cases, growth was unplanned. Fortunately The Staten Island Historical Society was farsighted and began in 1939 purchasing buildings of historical value in the Richmondtown area. With donations from friends, help from the City and a talent for overcoming obstacles, the Society has now acquired about 100 acres and many fine buildings.

Some of the buildings have been moved in from nearby locations and much work remains to be done to restore many of them. The ones that are open are delightful, the furnishings are a joy, and the museum collection is appealing to both children and adults. There is so much more tucked away in attics, including the fine quilt collection, waiting for the money and manpower to display it properly.

SILK GAME BOARD This Victorian silk quilt is not made from any one design but from at least three recognizable ones plus a lot of imagination. There are Caesar's Crowns and eight-pointed Stars and huge Sunbursts as well as some interesting diamond and striped borders. The silk is fine and fragile and its glowing colors have never faded. It was made in 1870 and recently presented to the Richmondtown Restoration where it is shown in the Lake Tysen House.

PINE TREE Pictorial designs are hard to create with squares and triangles but the makers of American piecework quilts succeeded in inventing several fine ones. The Pine Tree is an all-time favorite of this type and, though it originated in New England, it traveled to many other parts of the country. This one, in clear red and white, is shown in the Lake Tysen House at Richmondtown. It obviously had a hard life before being rescued and one end appears to have been nibbled by mice! What remains is a very excellent example of the Pine Tree pattern which you can find on pp. 59 & 60.

PINE TREE *Every square is pieced, all straight lines, but requiring more skill than the average beginner has.*

Each 13″ square (turned so as to be a diamond) contains 78 pieces. This single bed quilt originally contained 24 squares, four of them cut in half to go along the sides and another three cut across to fit in the top and bottom. The squares are set edge-to-edge, though this design is often seen with alternating white work squares.

Quilting is done diagonally in approximately 1″ squares. There is no border, only a red binding.

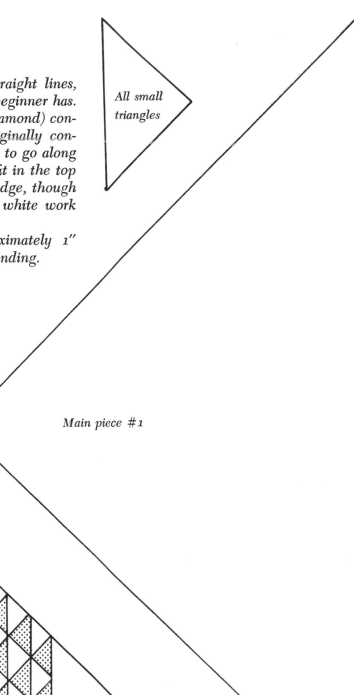

All small triangles

Main piece #1

Square #2

¼ size piecing diagram

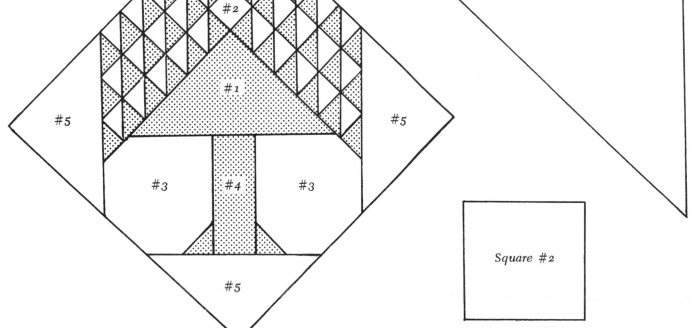

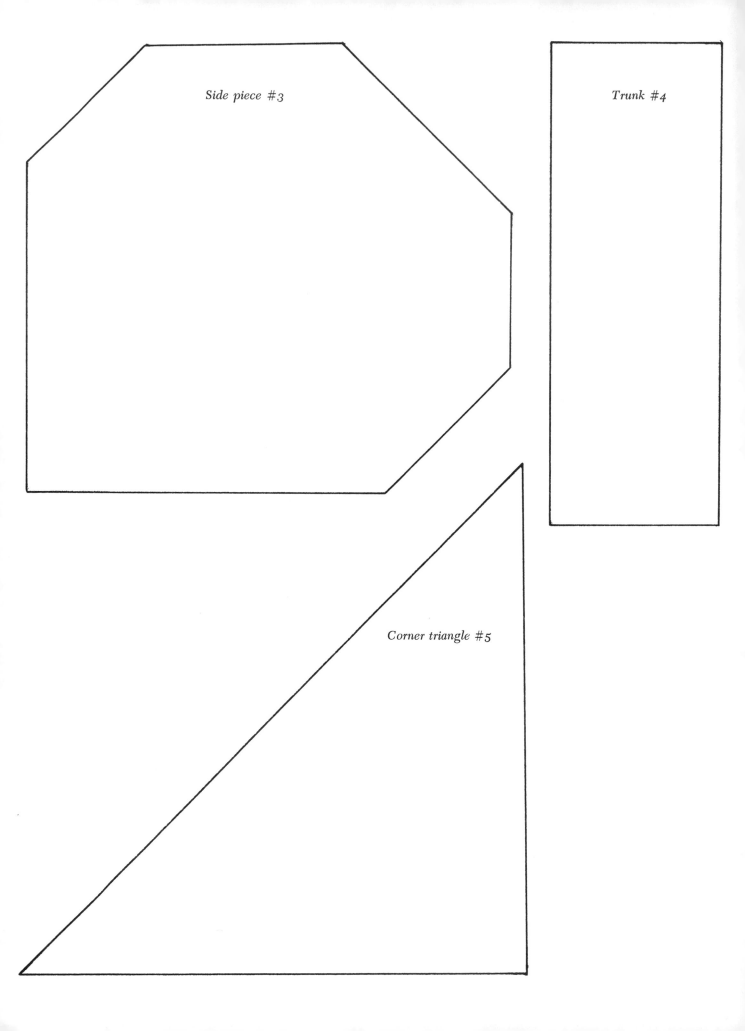

Side piece #3

Trunk #4

Corner triangle #5

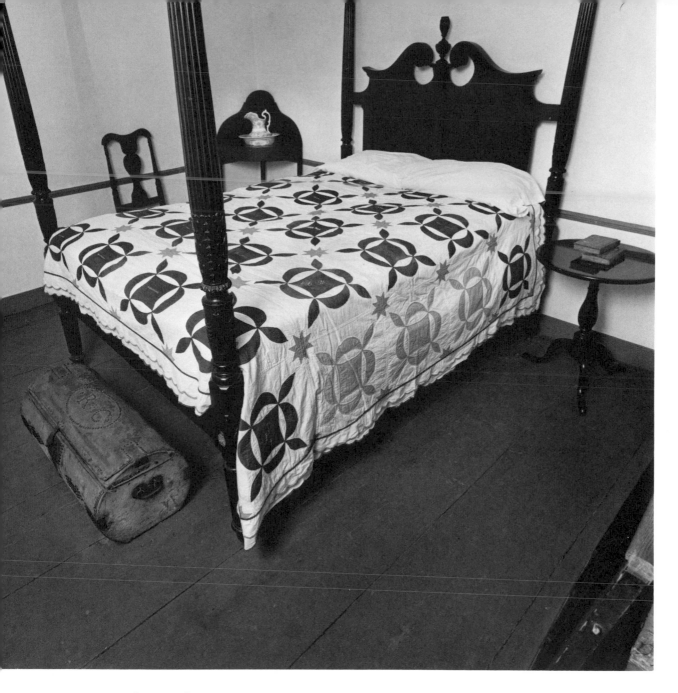

THE REEL   When Sophie Merrill married Abe Stoothoff on Staten Island in the 1860s, her friends made her a quilt and signed every block. We keep hearing of the superstition that required some squares in a quilt not to match because perfection is a dangerous thing for mortals to achieve. We're left to wonder whether that is the explanation for the tan fabric on the side, or did they simply run out, or did it fade because it was a different dye lot? The best feature of this quilt is the double layer border, scalloped and bound in orange to match the stars which were appliquéd on the intersections of the squares. For Reel diagram see pp. 62 & 63.

THE REEL   *The reel itself can be pieced or appliquéd. It is considered rather difficult in piecework because of the curves.*

Each of the 25 squares is 16″, set "edge-to-edge" with the star appliquéd on the intersections. If a smaller square were used, about 12″, the designs would meet and the effect would be quite interesting also.

The quilt is bound with a bias of the orange fabric and then two rows of scallops, on single layers of fabric, added. The scallop bands are about 3″ and 5″ wide and are separate, each bound narrowly with the orange.

¼ size piecing diagram

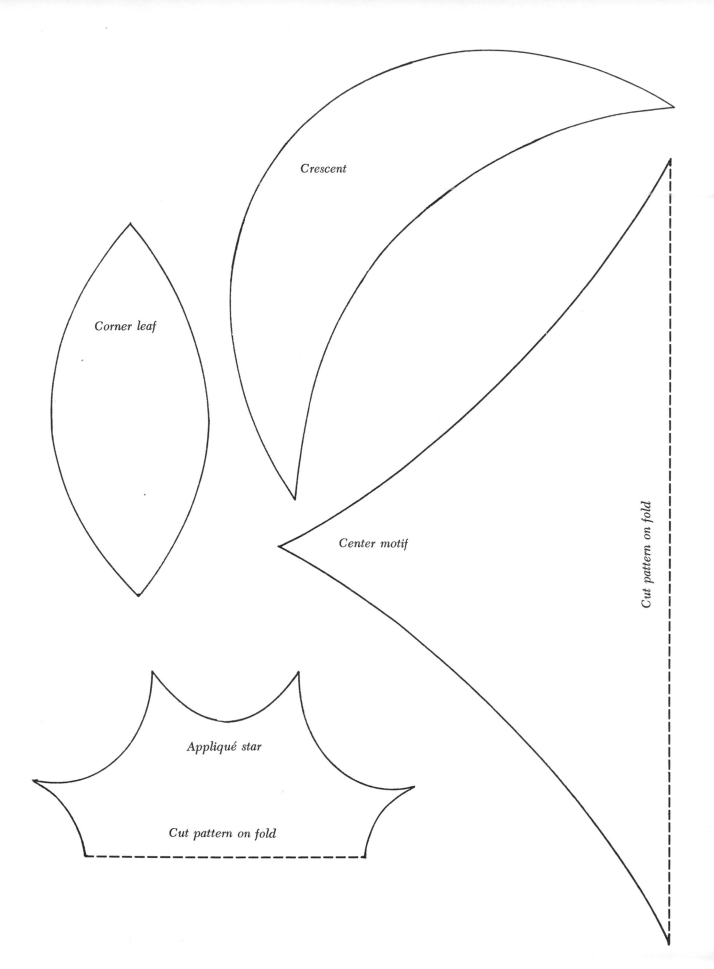

Crescent

Corner leaf

Center motif

Cut pattern on fold

Appliqué star

Cut pattern on fold

A family album quilt allows room for a great deal of imagination and all sorts of mementos as well as the more standard quilt designs. The trees and potted plants are typical of the time in which this Richmondtown quilt was made but the house is probably a replica of the family's own dwelling. The hand print was undoubtedly traced by one of the children in the family.

Children's art is always amusing for appliqué such as the series of horses and people seen here. The one at the far left might have been a Halloween figure. It seems possible that the quilt was many years in the making because of the small date on this section, thirteen years after the large date so boldly displayed on the other section.

BRONCK HOUSE
(*Museum of the Greene County Historical Society*)

In the lovely farmland between the Hudson River and the Catskills settled a sturdy race of farmers, homebuilders and civic minded people from Holland. Their fine stone houses seem as practical and livable today as when they were built in the 17th century. The first section of the Bronck House is just such a house, built by Pieter Bronck in 1663 and added to in 1685 as his family grew. In 1738 a more spacious house of brick was built next to the first one and later connected by an enclosed passageway. This became the prosperous home of Leonard Bronck, Greene County's first Judge of the Court of Common Pleas, 1800–1810.

Judge Bronck is responsible for the building of two other very interesting structures on the property. One has been called "The Stepmother's House," said to have been a necessity because his second wife and his grown daughters quarreled. This story has just about been proved to be untrue and the house is now thought to be a kitchen dependency. The other building is a wooden barn with thirteen sides, representing the thirteen colonies. It is said that Judge Bronck put thirteen slaves to work on it, starting on Friday the thirteenth. Considering how often wooden barns burned to the ground, he was obviously sure that superstitions were ridiculous! The barn stands bravely with many of the original timbers in it.

FLOWERS AND BIRDS   This finely designed and executed quilt came to the Bronck
House from the Spoor family of Coxsakie, New York. It is probably mid-nineteenth century and it is surely someone's masterpiece! The potted flowers are
similar to many used in that period, especially on album quilts. The quilting
and the border of birds and vines add the touch of a truly gifted needlewoman.
It is shown here in the large downstairs bedroom of the eighteenth century
part of the house. It is hardly necessary to have any other decoration in a room
where such a quilt is the central motif. See p. 68 for patterns.

Border leaf

FLOWERS AND BIRDS *The potted flowers are appliquéd on 14″ white squares, set alternately with quilted 14″ white squares. The flower stems are of bias fabric slightly less than ½″ wide.*

The border of padded grapes (size of a dime) and birds and leaves is 10″ wide plus 1¼″ red and white bands. The main vine is slightly over ½″ wide and the smaller stems slightly under. Both are cut of bias fabric.

The four-feather design on the white squares has a traditional Princess Feather treatment on the outer edge around rows of echo quilting. The remainder is filled with diamond design.

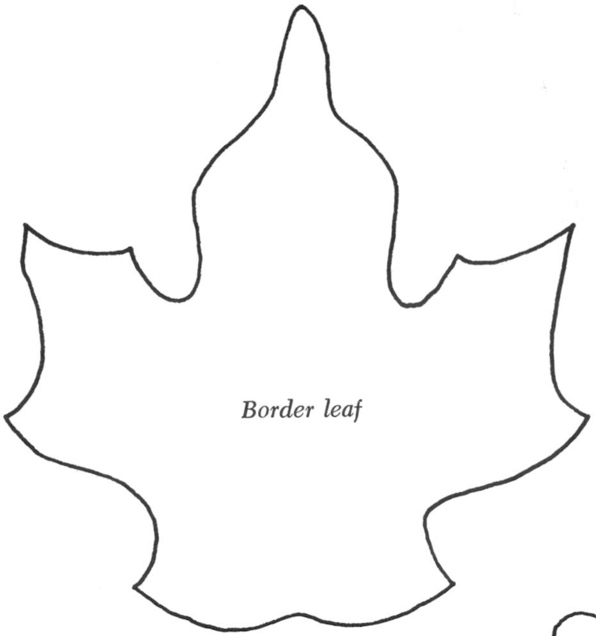

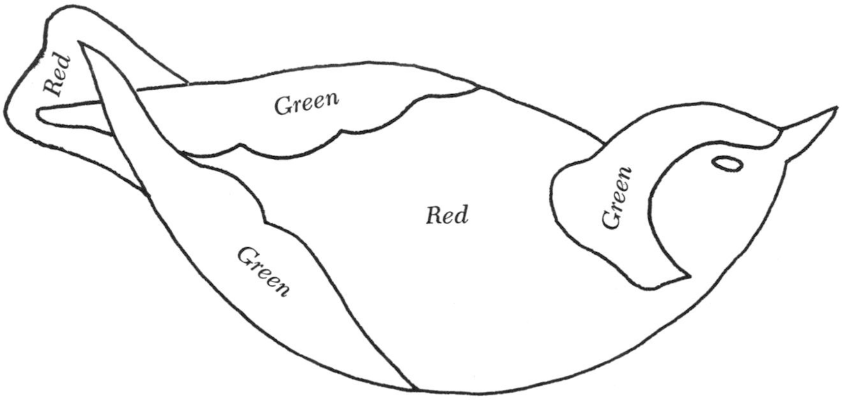

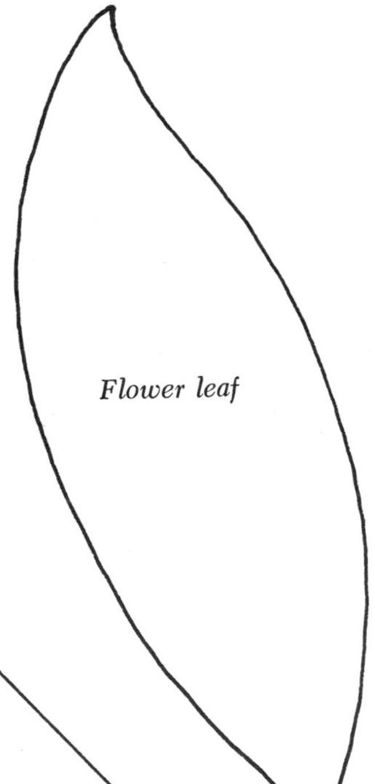

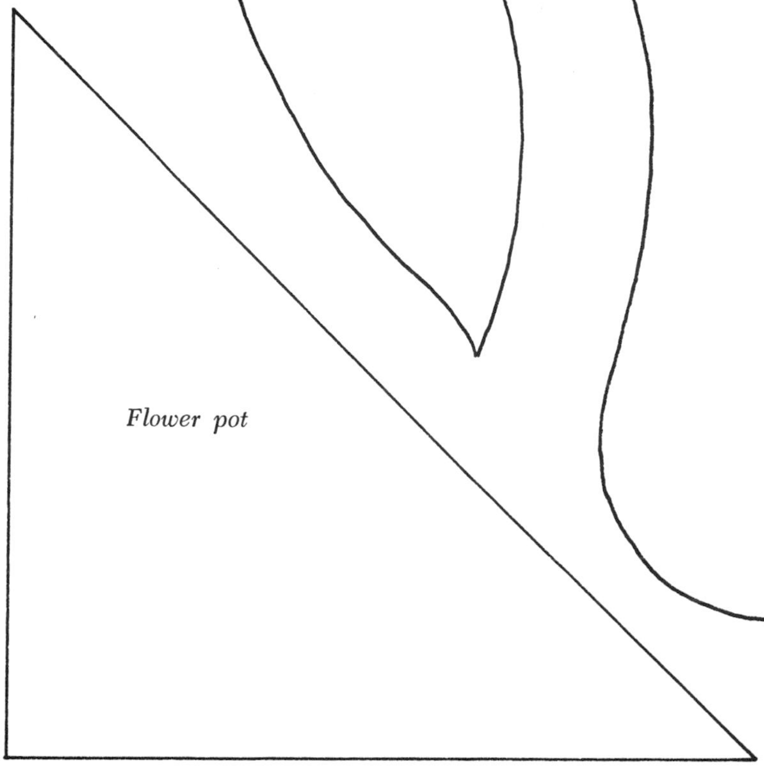

Red

Green

Green

Red

Green

Flower leaf

Flower pot

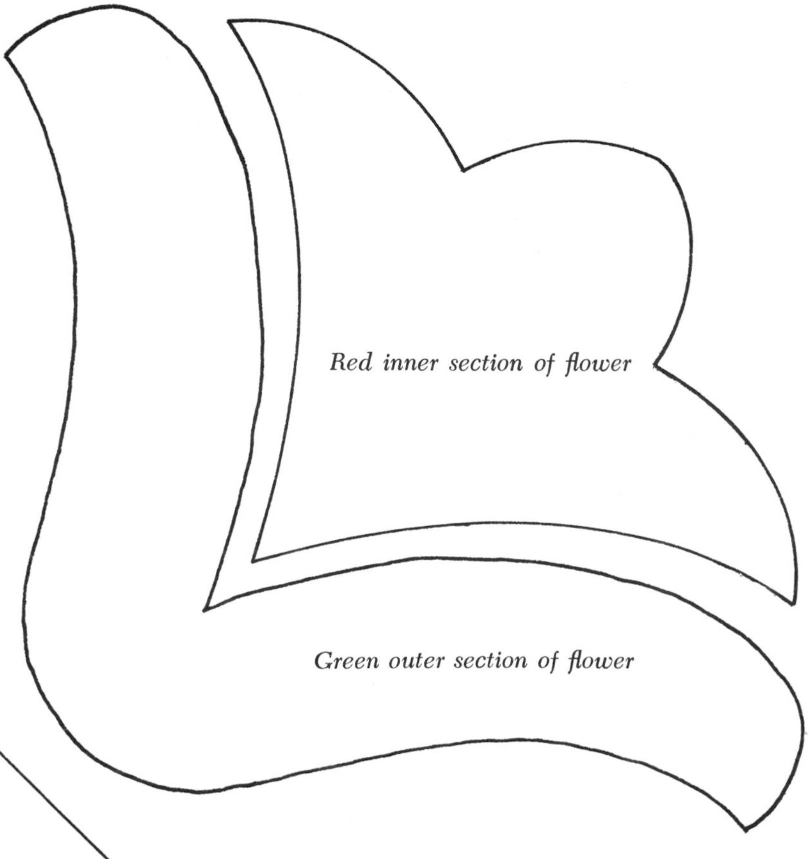

Red inner section of flower

Green outer section of flower

FLYING GEESE   One of the oldest and simplest piecework designs is Flying Geese, always made in stripes, usually alternating with solid colors. The same design is much used as a border, blending nicely with any pattern of squares or triangles. The one shown here in a tiny upstairs bedroom at Bronck House is a fine example, though beginning to show signs of disintegration. The back with its wide printed stripes is almost as nice as the top. The fabrics are 19th century calicoes and shirtings, now appearing to be all in brown tones, though they may originally have been more colorful. This is certainly one of the best and easiest designs for a beginner and is a perfect scrapbag quilt. Patterns and directions are on p. 70.

FLYING GEESE   *The geese form strips about 4¾" wide, alternated with 3¼" dark strips. The strips can be made in any length and as many as desired pieced together to form a quilt of the width desired.*

The back is pieced in alternating bands of light and dark print.

The quilting is in simple diamond design.

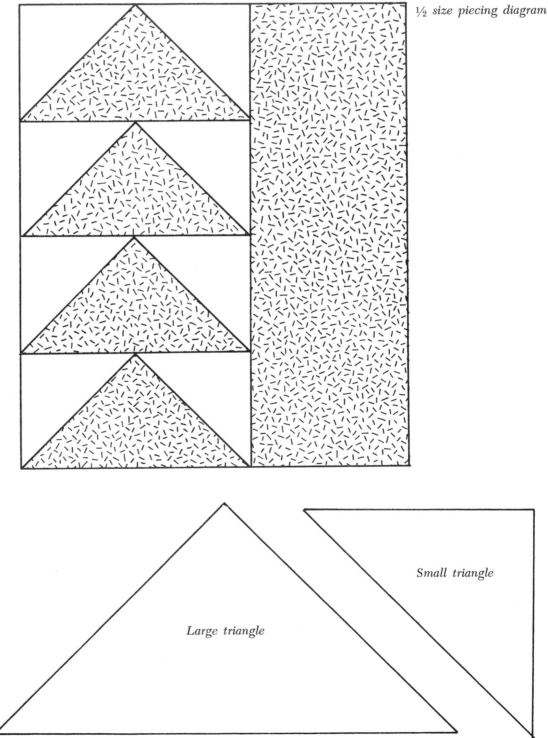

½ size piecing diagram

Large triangle

Small triangle

MONTAGE OF GEOMETRICS There are many fine quilts in the attic of Bronck House; three wonderfully easy and interesting geometric ones are shown here. In the left foreground is World Without End, in three shades of blue on white; next to it is Monkey Wrench or Double Monkey Wrench in red and white. Both of these were made by Catharine Dimmick and her daughter, Ora Dimmick Shaffer of Oneonta, New York. The little Snowball in the background was made by Mrs. George Griffin of Hendersonville, New York. The tiny polka dots in this navy and white quilt give it a properly wintry snowy appearance both for its name and for its area of the country. Diagrams and patterns are on pp. 72–75.

SNOWBALL   *The two-piece pattern is set edge-to-edge in alternating colors to form a Robbing Peter to Pay Paul design. It can be bordered and quilted as desired.*

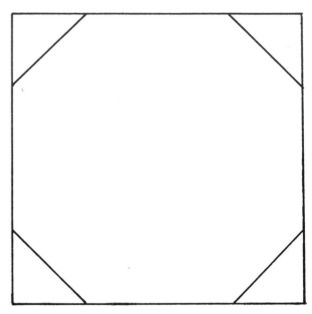

Full size pieces as arranged

MONKEY WRENCH *The red and white pieced design is set with 1½″ red and white bands and bordered with a red and a white 2″ band. The quilting outlines the pieces.*

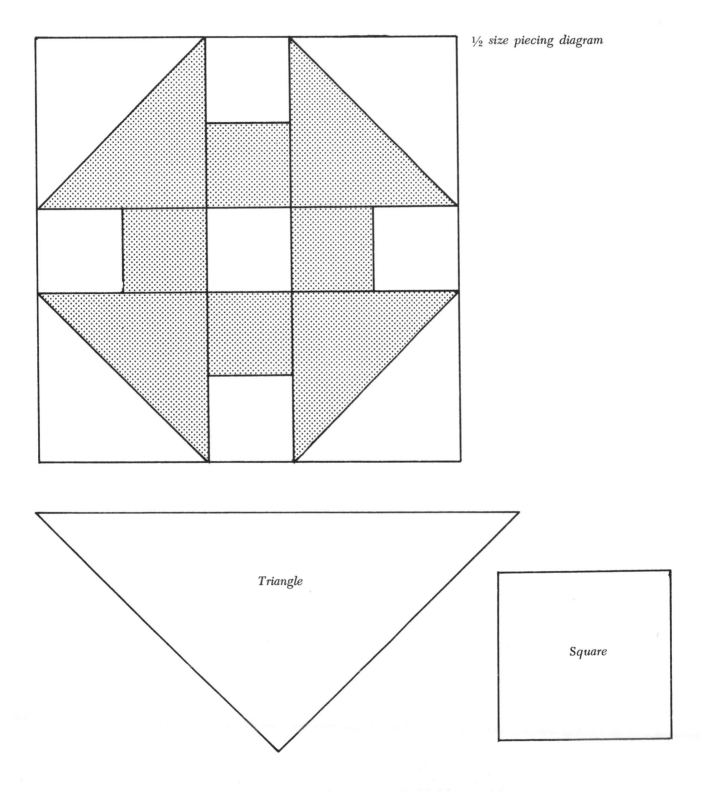

½ size piecing diagram

Triangle

Square

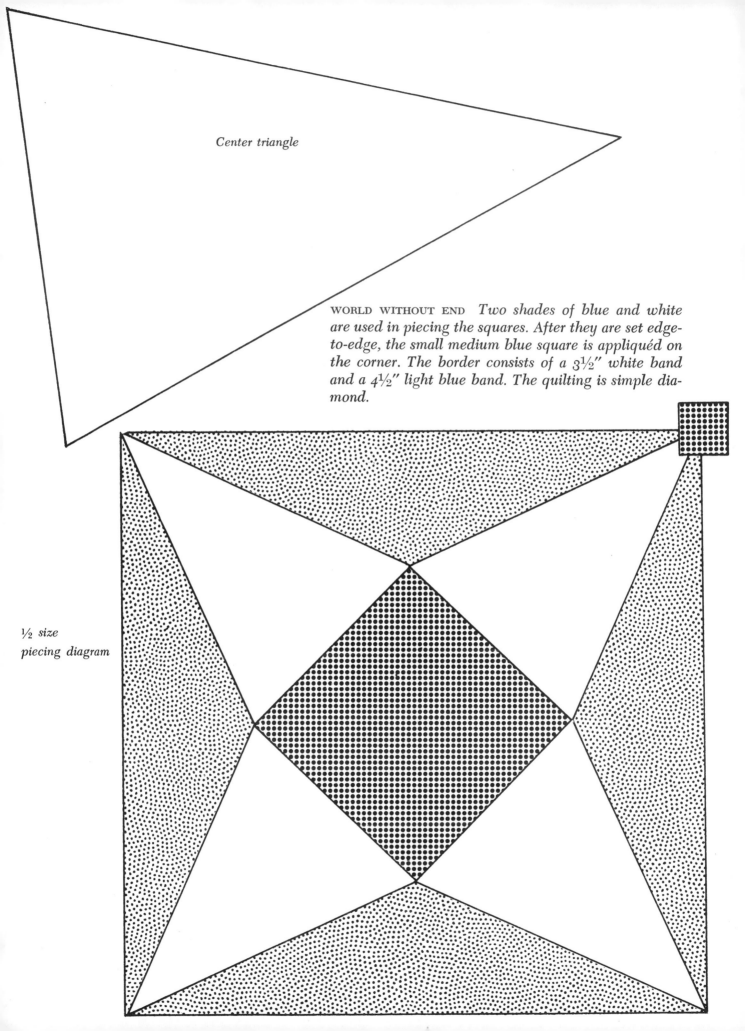

Center triangle

WORLD WITHOUT END *Two shades of blue and white are used in piecing the squares. After they are set edge-to-edge, the small medium blue square is appliquéd on the corner. The border consists of a 3½″ white band and a 4½″ light blue band. The quilting is simple diamond.*

½ size
piecing diagram

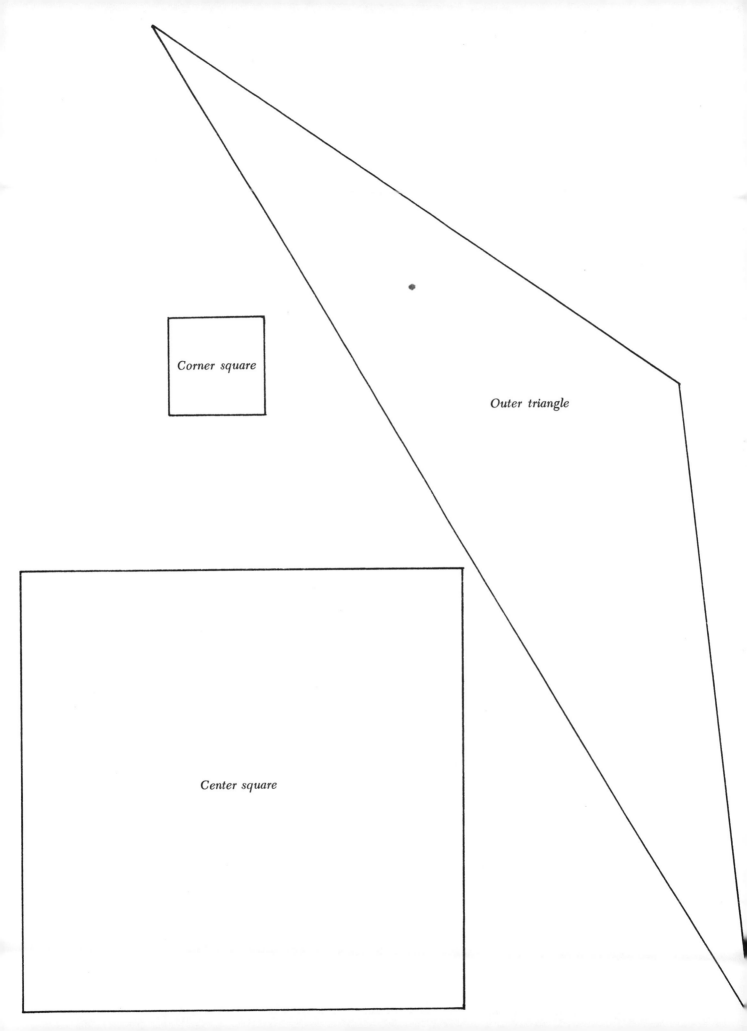

Corner square

Outer triangle

Center square

MORRISTOWN NATIONAL HISTORICAL PARK

There are many sections and two outstanding houses in this large rambling area in which so much Revolutionary history took place. The elegant Ford Mansion, built in 1774, was Washington's Headquarters in 1779–80. A few miles away, on the edge of Jockey Hollow, is the modest 1750 farmhouse built by Henry Wick and also occupied by Continental Army officers. The Wick Farm was the scene of a mutiny by ill-clothed and ill-fed troops stationed in Jockey Hollow in 1781.

Both houses are beautifully restored and furnished in the manner of the time that they were built. There are relics of the Revolution and its heroes in the houses and in a large museum building near the Ford Mansion. It is particularly interesting to see the two houses on the same day and compare the ways of life of two families of the eighteenth century, one in comfortable circumstances and one wealthy. The gardens at the Wick House make a spring visit especially pleasant.

SIMPLE STAR Sometime before 1800 this Simple Star quilt was pieced of linsey-woolsey, which had undoubtedly served another purpose before being cut and worked into such a charming bed cover. The cut-out for the bed post, a very sensible arrangement, appears less and less after 1800 and linsey-woolsey was rejected by most quilters for more colorful and dainty fabrics. The colors were originally the mossy green that still makes up a large part of the quilt and probably a dark pink or light red which has faded and in many spots been replaced with cotton sateen and other later fabrics. Much of the crewel embroidery is original but that, too, has some lines worked in newer thread. It is photographed on the master bed in the Wick House, where it can be seen. Patterns and suggestions are on p. 78.

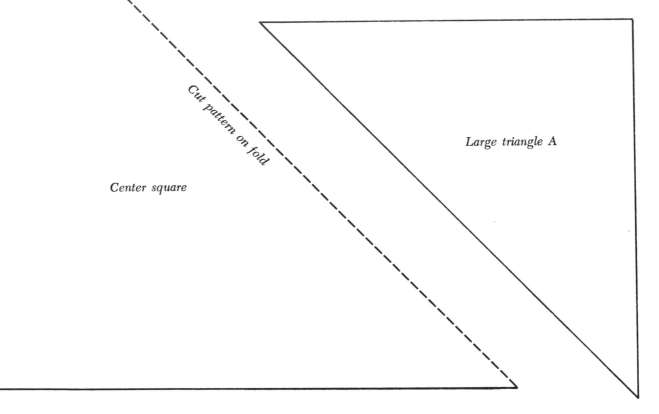

Small triangle B

SIMPLE STAR   *The Star squares are pieced and alternated with solid squares, 11″ on each side. Two or three colors can be used throughout or scrap pieces can be used for the points of the star.*

The quilting is done in straight line but in alternating directions on alternating squares. The solid squares are decorated with flower designs in crewel work. This quilt could be very effectively made of a hard finish wool or coarse cotton or linen.

Cut pattern on fold

Large triangle A

Center square

¼ size piecing diagram

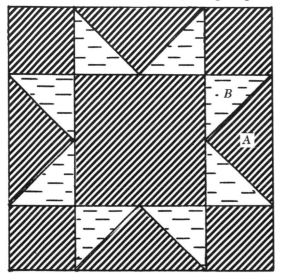

· B

A

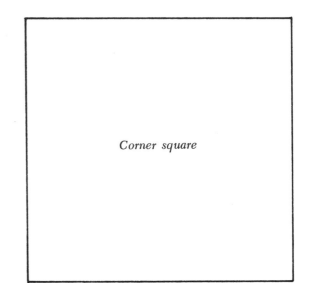

Corner square

GERMANTOWN HISTORICAL SOCIETY

There is a museum complex in the heart of Germantown, Philadelphia, Pennsylvania, that does for city living of the past what the Pennsylvania Farm Museum does for farm living. It is comprised of a group of houses representative of the way Germantown looked before the bulldozer and the wrecker's ball began to make 20th century "improvements." It was started in 1900 by a group of citizens who saw the grim handwriting on the wall and rescued some extremely handsome buildings on Germantown Avenue. Germantown as early as 1690 had a reputation for its production of linen and its famous "Germantown stockings," and remained one of the colonies' most important textile centers through the nineteenth century.

From the quilters' point of view this is a real treasure trove as there is one house devoted to quilts and toys, with an extensive collection of both. For lovers of textiles of all kinds there is also a costume museum in another building. As is the case with so many museum complexes and villages, new things are happening all the time and additions are being made to collections.

SAW TOOTH   If ever there was a design that could be executed by anyone who'd ever dreamed of making a quilt and in any assortment of scrapbag pieces, the single Saw Tooth is it. It can also, through its use of color and fine stitchery, become a worthy museum piece. This one is a Friendship quilt, made in 1849, and not only signed, but decorated with tiny sketches and mottos in the white triangles. It is shown in the Howell House of the Germantown Historical Society, where it is on display in a collection of many fine quilts. The pattern is on p. 80.

SAW TOOTH *This is a pieced quilt, all straight line pieces, perfect for a beginner. It can be made in two colors or in one color, or white and scrapbag pieces. Ample room is allowed for signatures or other embroidery.*

Nine by ten squares will make a 72" x 80" quilt. It has no border as seen here but can be finished with 3" bands of predominant colors.

The quilting follows the outlines of the piecing, but small white work designs could be done in the large triangles instead of other embroideries or writing.

Large triangle

Small triangle

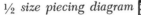

½ *size piecing diagram*

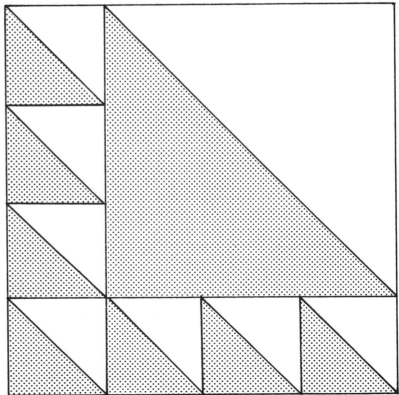

BASKET AND ROSE   The use of two quite different patterns in alternating squares can produce a most harmonious effect as in this quilt on the frame in the attic of the Conyngham-Hacker House in Germantown. The Basket pattern, a long time favorite with many variations, is half pieced and half appliquéd. The Rose, sometimes known as Rose of Sharon, is appliquéd. The design is worked so that the baskets are upright when viewed from either side of the bed or from the bottom, almost like a border. The colors of the flowers are traditional, pink and green, but the baskets are a strong blue and white with beige handles, all of which blends surprisingly well. Both patterns, to be used together or separately, can be found on pp. 82 & 83.

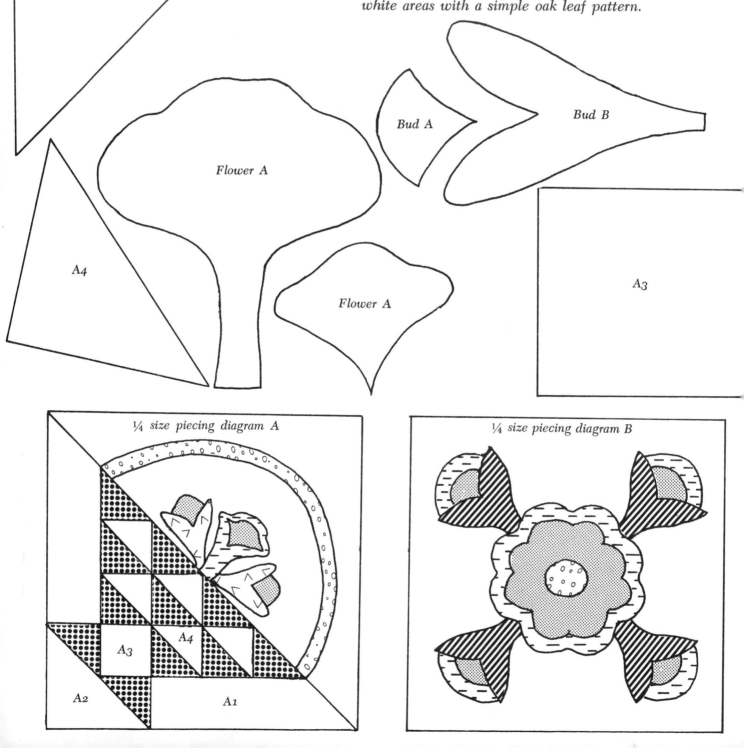

A2

A4

Flower A

Bud A

Bud B

Flower A

A3

BASKET AND ROSE *The basket squares are half pieced and half appliquéd. The white triangle on which the handle and flowers are appliquéd is 13″ along each side, matching in size the pieced triangle. The Rose of Sharon is entirely appliquéd on a 13″ white square.*

The quilt could be finished with an appliquéd border or with a border in bands of color. The quilting is minimal, outlining the pieces and filling the white areas around the baskets in straight lines and the other white areas with a simple oak leaf pattern.

¼ size piecing diagram A

A4

A3

A2

A1

¼ size piecing diagram B

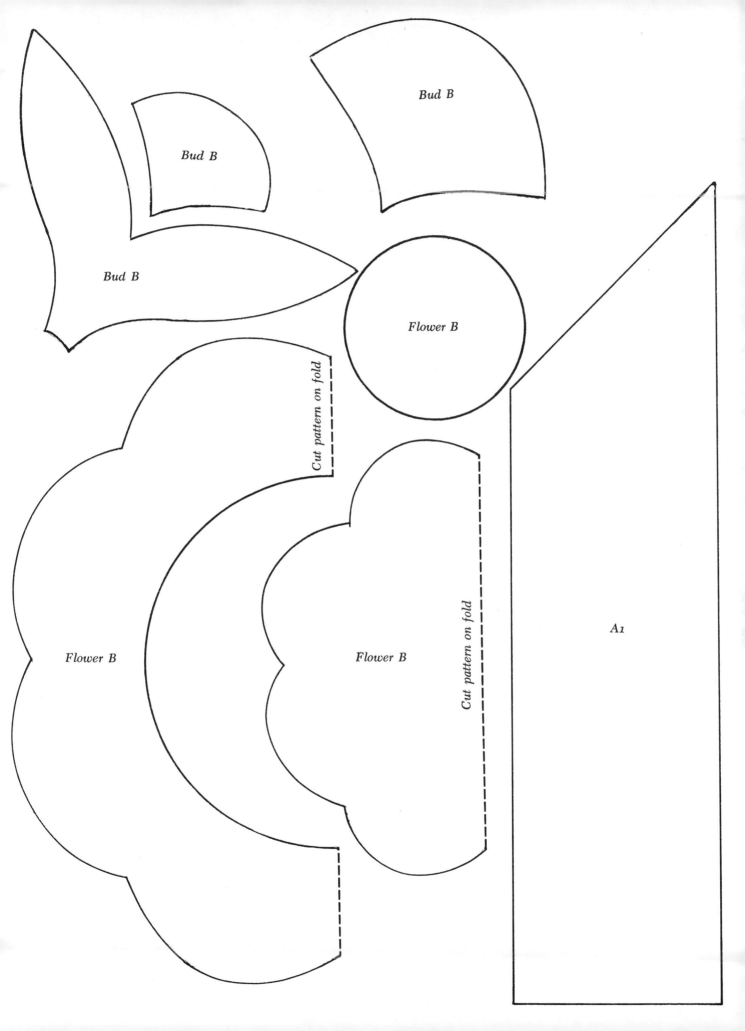

Bud B

Bud B

Bud B

Flower B

Cut pattern on fold

Flower B

Flower B

Cut pattern on fold

A1

HEARTS ALL AROUND When it comes to making quilts, there seem to be people who like piecing the tops and people who like quilting. Apparently even back in 1830 the same thing was true because a lady in Germantown pieced and probably designed this marvelous top but never finished it. From the standpoint of a museum, that has a great advantage because it also never was used and so is in very good condition. The design, all done in navy with tiny white dots, comes together in the corners so as to make a second pattern, giving almost an effect of alternating squares. This quilt is on display in the Howell House in Germantown. Patterns are on pp. 85 & 86.

HEARTS ALL AROUND *The entire design is appliquéd in one color onto 16″ white squares. The squares are then joined edge-to-edge to form a double pattern.*

The border is 10″ wide with vines and stems formed of 1½″ and ⅝″ bias. The edges should be finished with narrow white bias binding.

It would not be necessary to do more than outline quilting around the designs, though a repeat of hearts in the white areas would be true to the style.

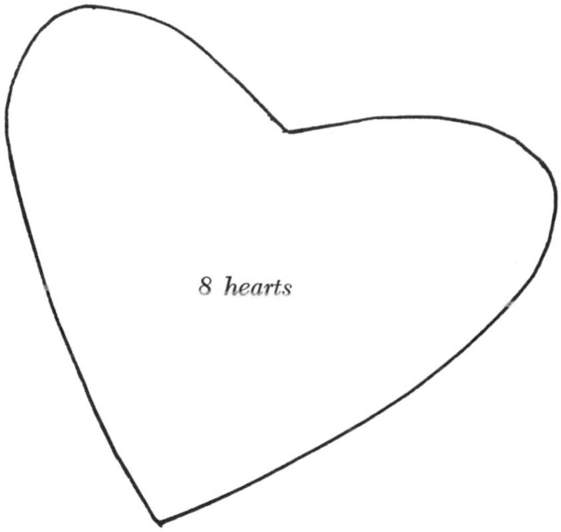

8 hearts

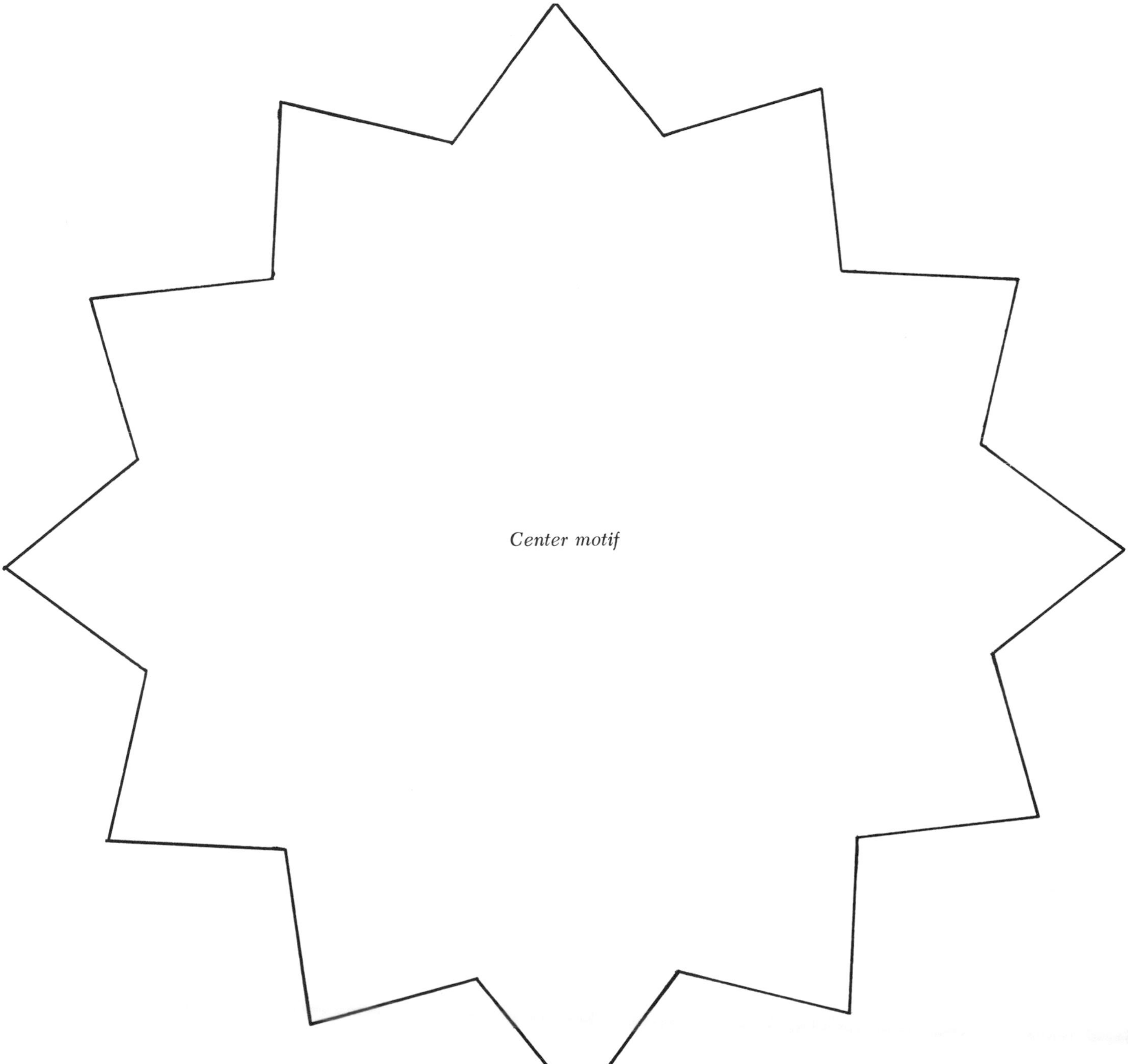

Center motif

Border #1

Border #2

Border #3

Corner heart and leaf

PENNSYLVANIA FARM MUSEUM

The life of the early settlers in any community changed slowly, leaving behind houses and crafts and professions of several generations blending smoothly together in one locality. The Pennsylvania Farm Museum keeps its realistic flavor by preserving a group of structures of the eighteenth and nineteenth century and keeping them alive with people spinning and weaving and cooking just as they would have done in those times. Everything there has a feeling of being alive and lived in and functioning. The complex is still growing and the farmland being developed and used more fully. Eventually it will encompass all phases of farming and farm life in Pennsylvania. It has fine and growing collections of quilts and cooking utensils, farm equipment and furniture, looms and hand tools, and all the other bits and pieces of farmlife as it was lived in the Landis Valley. There is something of interest to be found there by people of every age and background.

1843 FRIENDSHIP QUILT   In many ways this quilt defies description or categorizing; it is an Album quilt or a Friendship quilt, depending on your point of view, and it is an entire history of quilting. There are cutout appliqués, traditional appliqué designs such as the Sunburst and delightful patchwork variations, mostly nine patch. Any one of the patterns can be used for a whole quilt; most of them are easy enough for a beginner to do and the majority of them are fine friendship designs because of the large white space in the center.

Mothers shouldn't have favorite children and the same can be said of authors, but this is the quilt that we return to again and again. It is in the collection of The Pennsylvania Farm Museum and was photographed there with some of the museum buildings showing in the background. Even the clothespins are museum artifacts. See pp. 88–95 for details and patterns.

No. 1 Sunburst

No. 2 St. Andrew's Cross

No. 3 Double Cross or Pyramid

No. 4 Checkerboard

No. 5 Oak Leaves

No. 6 Friendship Heart

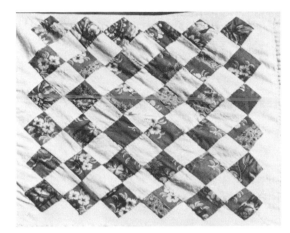

No. 7 Small Diagonal Checkerboard

No. 8 Criss Cross

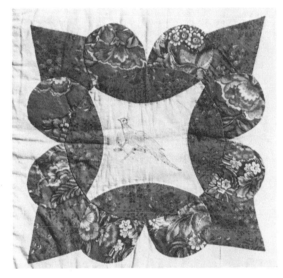

No. 9 Friendship Frame

No. 10 Friendship Leaf

No. 11 Orange Peel or Reel

No. 12 Ohio Star

No. 13 Christian Cross

No. 14 Nine Patch

No. 15 Friendship Star

1843 FRIENDSHIP QUILT *Some squares are pieced and some appliquéd, as can be seen in detail photography. Each square is 11″, seven squares in each direction. Many patterns are suitable for use separately in the manner of the Puss in the Corner quilt, p. 116. Pattern pieces are keyed to detail photographs.*

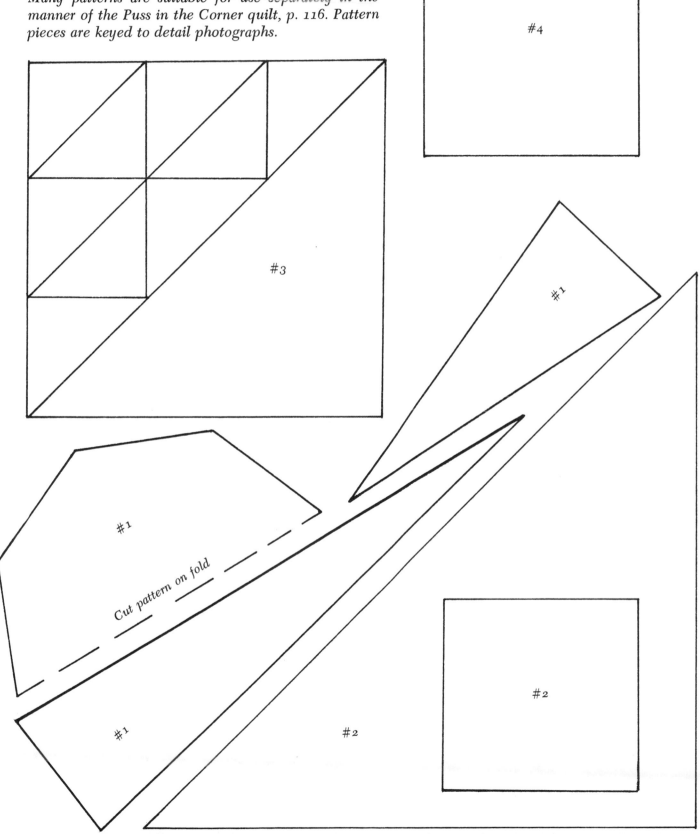

#4

#3

#1

#1

Cut pattern on fold

#1

#2

#2

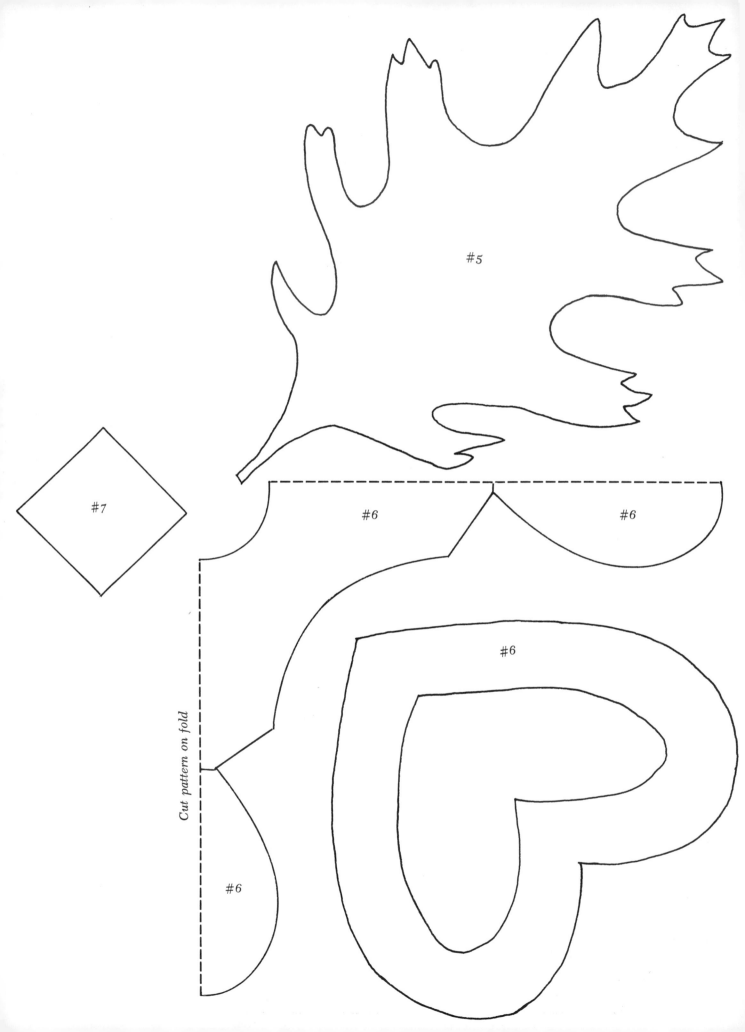

#5

#7

#6

#6

#6

#6

Cut pattern on fold

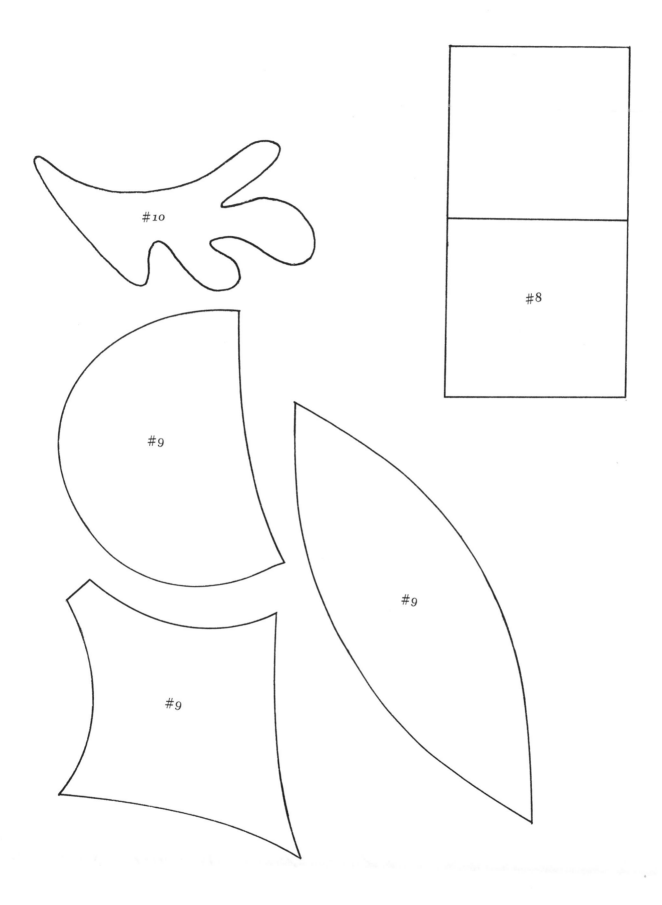

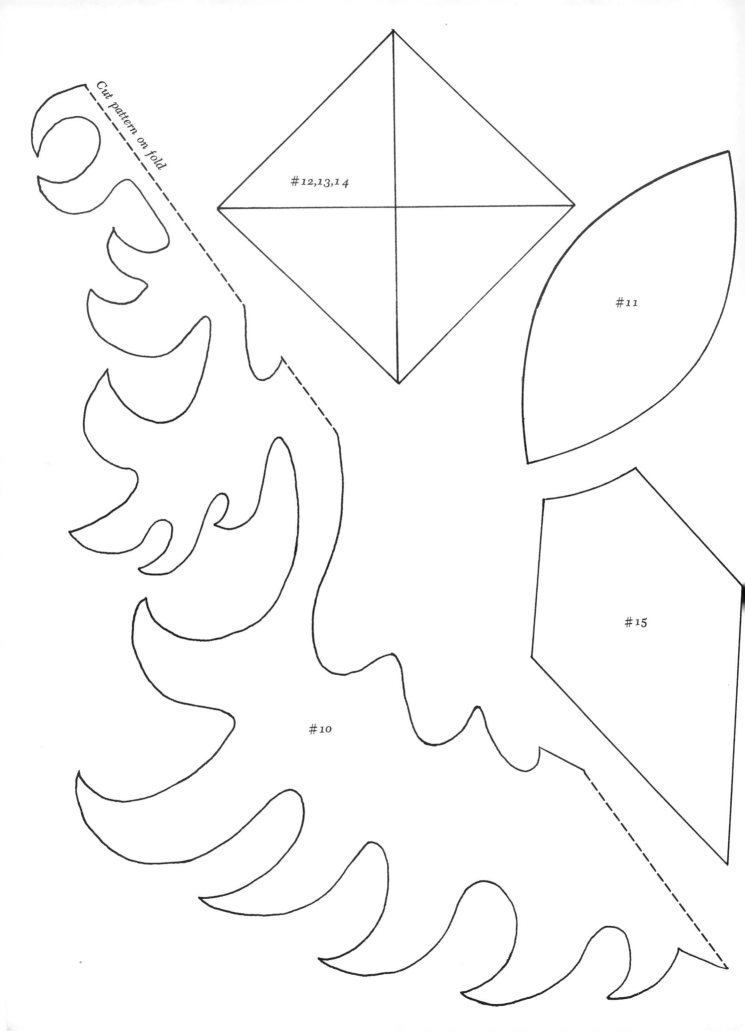

Cut pattern on fold

#12,13,14

#11

#15

#10

Cut pattern on fold

Alternate #10

CUT-PAPER COCKSCOMB A handsome quilt of Pennsylvania origin is made in the cut-paper style of so-called Hawaiian quilts. Paper folding and cutting is seen in the folk art of many lands so it is not surprising that it appears in the designs of quilts and other needlework all over the world. There are some fairly typical Pennsylvania German touches to this quilt, including the bright pink and green coloring and the hearts inside the large flowers. The setting is the Pennsylvania Farm Museum, which boasts many fine quilts in its permanent collection, including this one. You will find patterns, dimensions and suggestions for this quilt on pp. 97–99.

CUT-PAPER COCKSCOMB *The center of the quilt is appliquéd onto one 60" white square. This and the intricacy of the border make a quilt suitable for the more experienced quilter.*

The borders are 14" wide. For the center panel cut bias strips for the stems, four 8" x ¾", four 20½" x 1" and eight 9½" x ¾". Cut a quantity of ⅜" bias for the stems in the border. Between the center panel and the wide border is a 3" Saw Tooth border of green and white.

The quilting in the large border, the center motif and the hearts is done in a ½" diamond. The large white areas are quilted with leaves, flowers and circles, as are the larger appliquéd pieces.

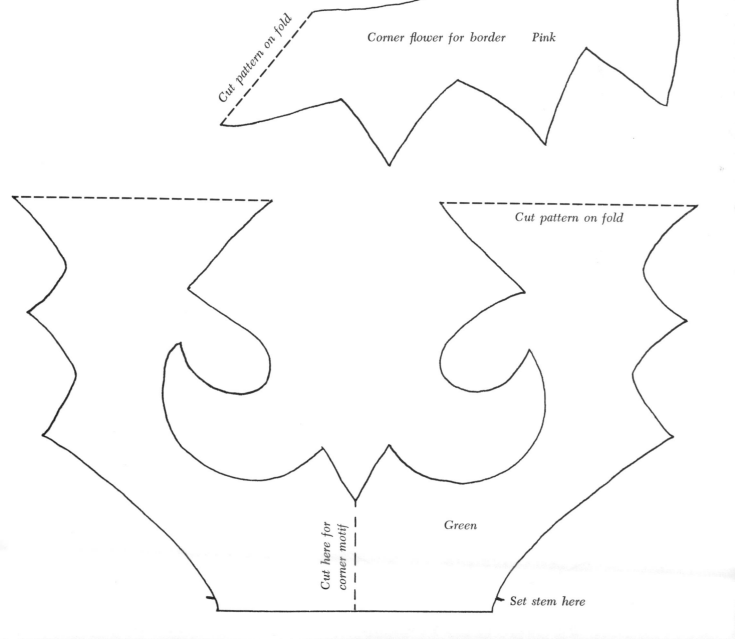

Cut pattern on fold

Corner flower for border   Pink

Cut pattern on fold

Cut here for corner motif

Green

Set stem here

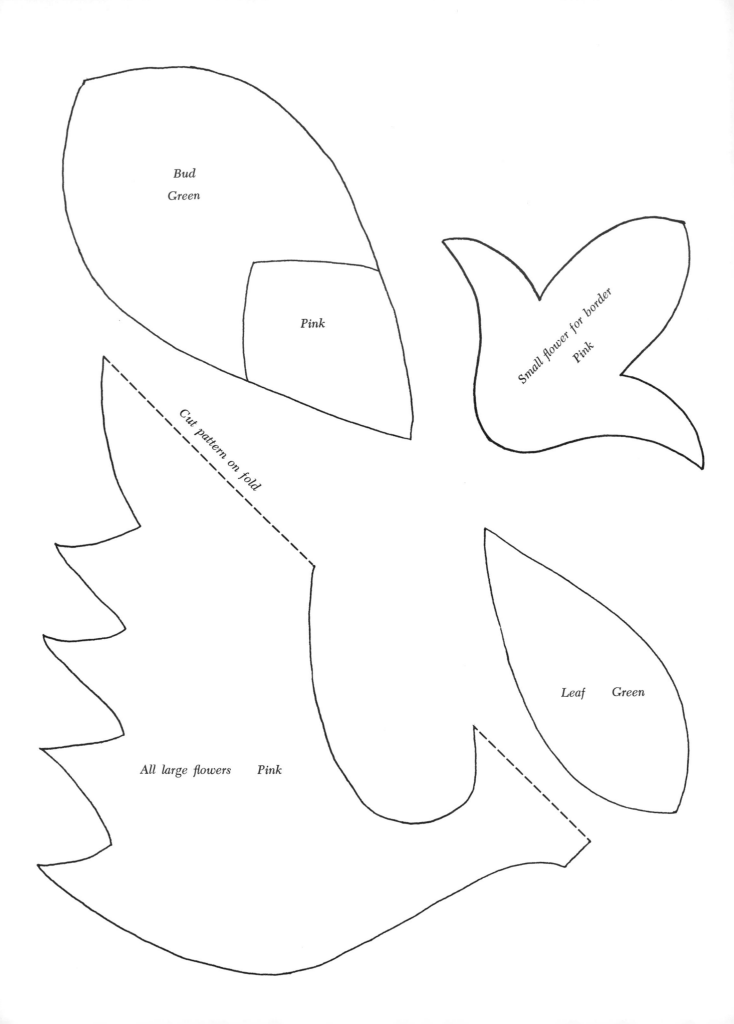

Bud

Green

Pink

Small flower for border

Pink

Cut pattern on fold

Leaf   Green

All large flowers   Pink

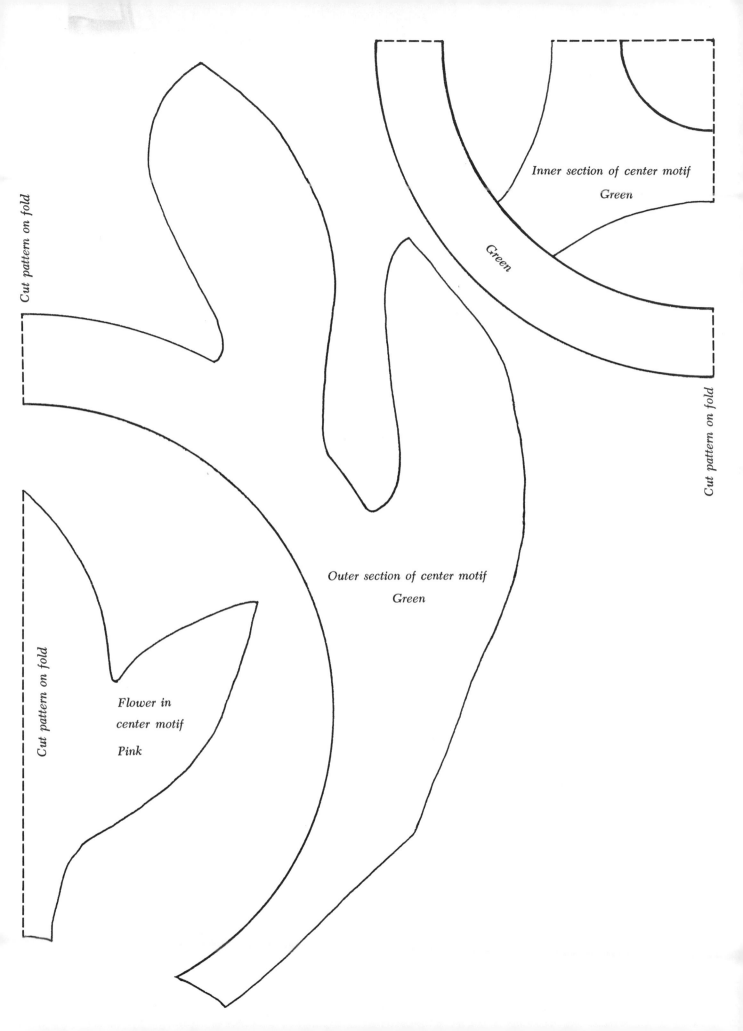

Cut pattern on fold

Inner section of center motif

Green

Green

Cut pattern on fold

Outer section of center motif

Green

Cut pattern on fold

Flower in
center motif
Pink

THISTLE CRIB QUILT No sentimental pink and blue nursery design but a bold colorful floral was worked before 1850 for a hearty Pennsylvania German baby. This quilt, in sharp pink and green with a surprising touch of orange, is most certainly related to the Giant Tulip one on p. 102. The uncluttered practicality of the farm house nursery was cheered and brightened by the addition of such original designs. In rooms where few pictures hung on the clean white walls and there was no overabundance of toys and decoration, the quilt emerges as a real work of folk art. The design will make the transition from the Pennsylvania Farm Museum to any twentieth century nursery and become, once again, the very first piece of art to be appreciated by a very small child. Patterns on pp. 101 & 102.

THISTLE CRIB QUILT *The design is appliquéd on a 32″ white square. The alternating pink and green triangles in the Saw Tooth border are made from 2½″ squares cut across. The white border is 5½″, making the total quilt size 48″ square.*

In the original the pot and the corner flowers are made of a dark green calico print. The other leaves and stems are a bright solid green. Cut the main stem of bias, 12½″ x 1¼″, in pink; it is not laid on straight but curved slightly for a more graceful effect.

Quilting is done around all appliqué pieces and in 1″ squares over the white part of the center. The border is quilted in diamonds with the lines 1″ apart.

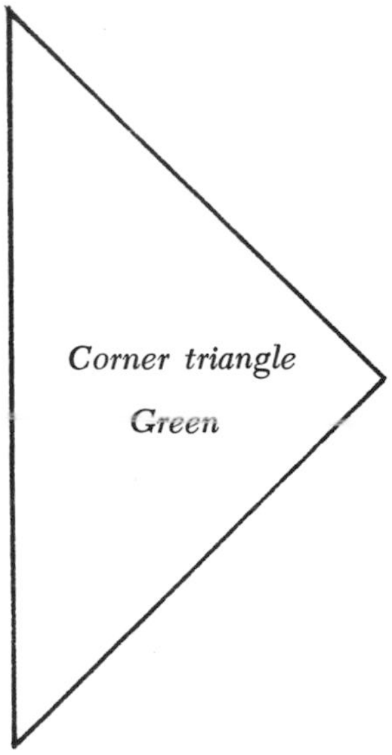

Corner triangle

Green

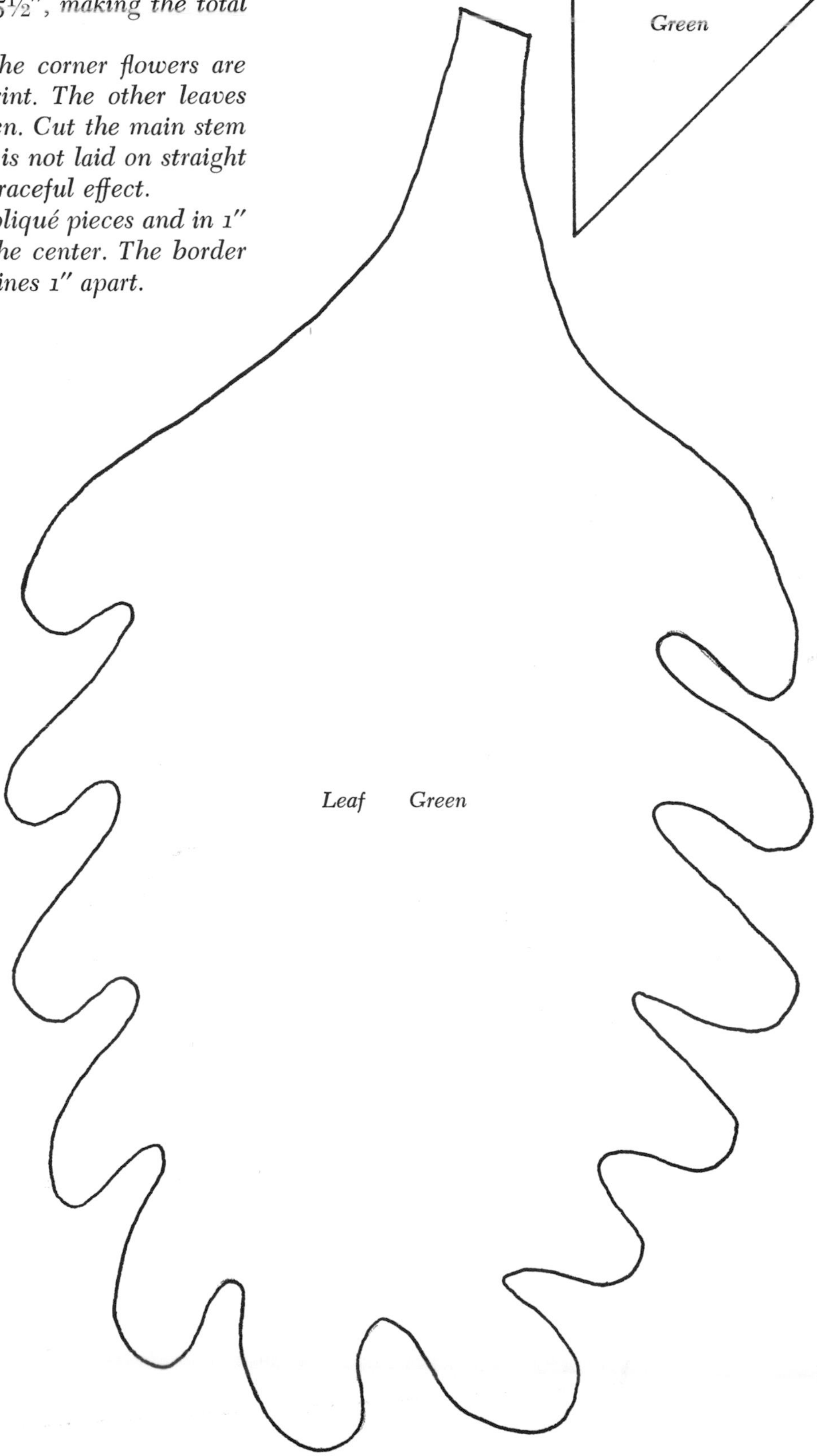

Leaf   Green

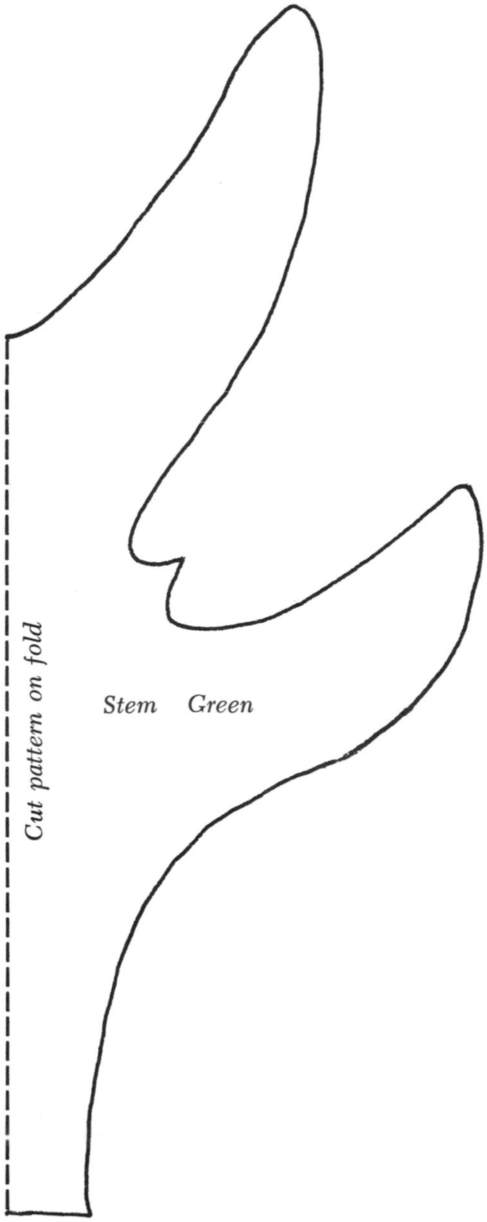

Stem   Green

Cut pattern on fold

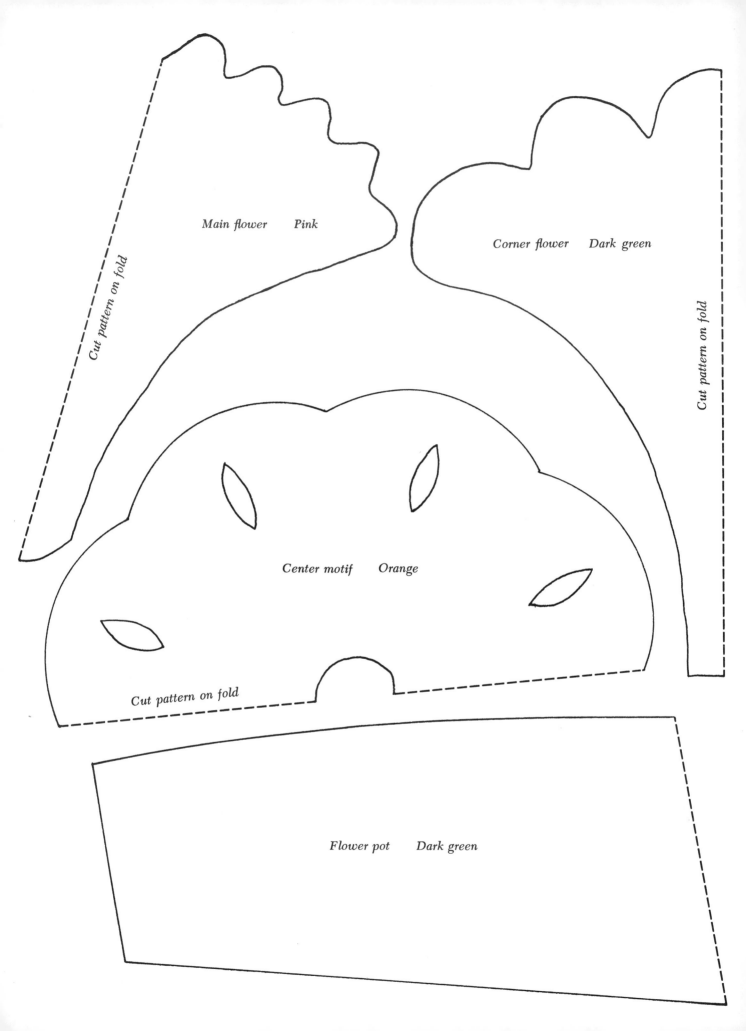

Main flower   Pink

Corner flower   Dark green

Cut pattern on fold

Cut pattern on fold

Center motif   Orange

Cut pattern on fold

Flower pot   Dark green

GIANT TULIP We speak of Modern design and Early American design as though the two have nothing in common. Many of the mid-nineteenth century Pennsylvania German quilts are forerunners of Modern but are completely compatible with their whitewashed Early American farm houses. The designs were often based on flowers, often highly original and usually made in vibrant colors on a bold scale. It is quite probable that this Tulip quilt and the Thistle crib quilt were from the same hand or the same family. The fabrics are of the same quality and the colors in both are bright pink and green with a touch of orange as a small shocking accent. The handwork on both, including this fine white work border, is excellent. They are in the Pennsylvania Farm Museum and were photographed there in the 1815 House. Diagram on pp. 104–107.

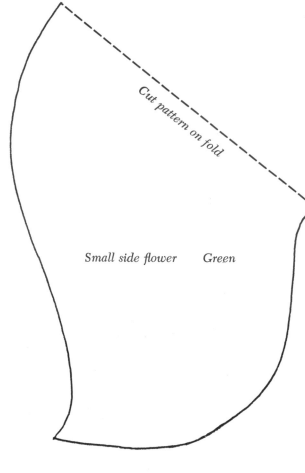

Cut pattern on fold

Small side flower   Green

GIANT TULIP *The design is appliquéd on four 32"
squares. The connecting borders are bright pink, 1½"
wide. The outer white border is 11" wide, handsomely
quilted. The large smooth outline and the fact that
there are only four squares to complete make this a
good first quilt in appliqué.*

*Cut straight pieces 10" x 1¼" in green for the large
flower stems and 6¾" x 1" in green for the small flower
stems. It may be especially wise to back and stabilize
the pieces with a thin iron-on or non-woven interfacing
because of their unusually large size which makes it
easier to stretch them out of shape.*

*The quilting is done around the designs and elab-
orately in the border by a design found on pp. 106 &
107.*

*Reduced in half this design could be handled in a
different manner with wider connecting borders or sets
and a narrower outer border. It also makes a fine design for the top of a 16" pillow.*

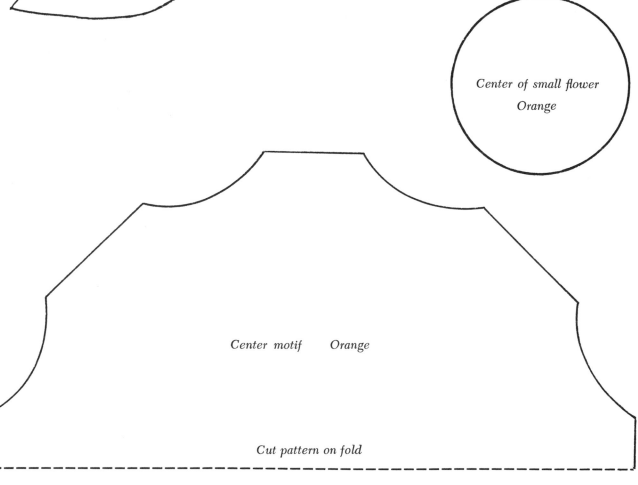

Center of small flower
Orange

Center motif   Orange

Cut pattern on fold

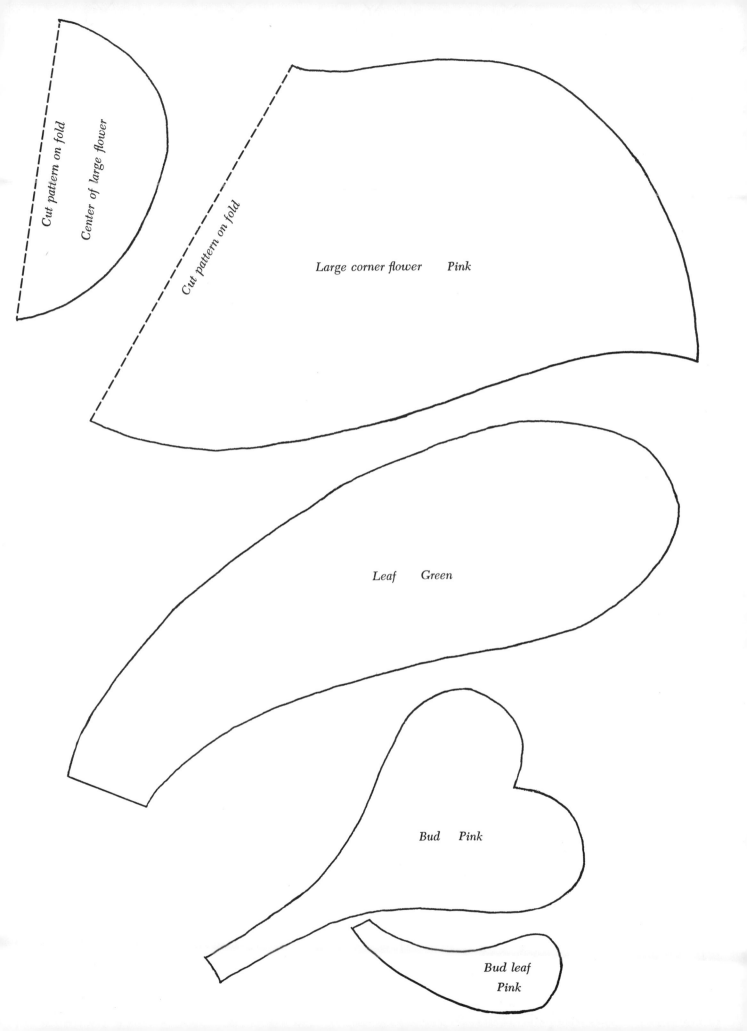

Cut pattern on fold

Center of large flower

Cut pattern on fold

Large corner flower   Pink

Leaf   Green

Bud   Pink

Bud leaf

Pink

THE KEMERER MUSEUM

The private collector has done much to preserve local art that might otherwise have vanished from sight. Such a woman was Annie S. Kemerer, who collected locally made clocks, folk art, and some very fine glass as well as Oriental rugs and furniture from all the world. There are quilts from her own family and other local ones that have been added to the collection. Many are on display at all times.

She left her entire collection to form the nucleus of the museum for Bethlehem, Pennsylvania, and the Lehigh Valley, where it is now housed in a fine nineteenth century house. The whole effect is of a period of gracious living in the home of a person who knew how to choose the best. Many other fortunate towns are realizing the value of such small local museums run with the aid and time of the people in the community.

CROWN As in so many cases with quilt designs, this is not quite like any named pattern; it is a bit like Caesar's Crown, but not so elaborate, it is a distant cousin of Robbing Peter to Pay Paul. In the end we feel that it is a wonderful colorful expression of the artistic talent of Mary Bachman Kemerer, who made it over 100 years ago. The white work is superb and there is such good optical illusion in the double pattern that the edge-to-edge setting creates. It is displayed here in the Kemerer Museum and can be seen there along with other fine quilts and folk art of the Pennsylvania German community. For patterns see pp. 109–112.

CROWN *The whole square may be pieced or the center, omitting the white corner piece, can be pieced and appliquéd on a 16" white square. If you plan to piece the entire square, you might find it easier to cut the crown itself in four pieces, instead of making the pattern on the folds.*

The white work border is 11" wide, flanked by the two pieced borders. The motifs given for the white work are only partial and are included as suggestions to which you may add your own.

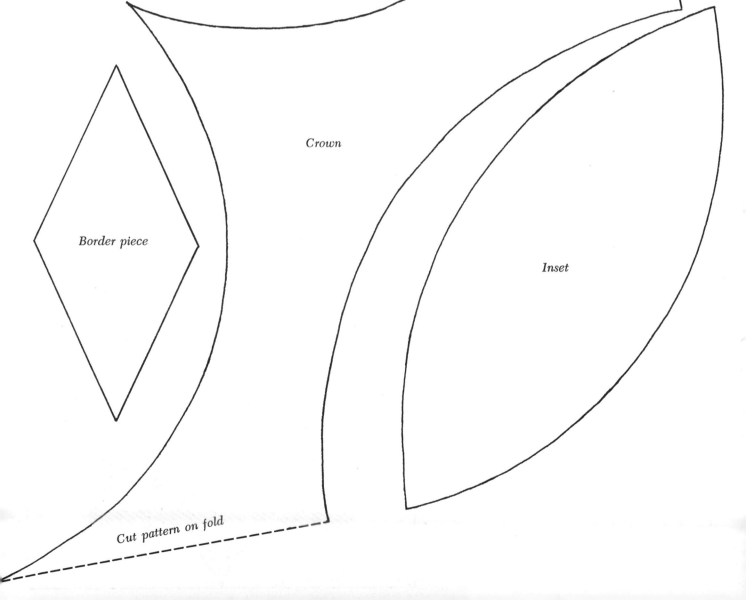

Crown

Border piece

Inset

Cut pattern on fold

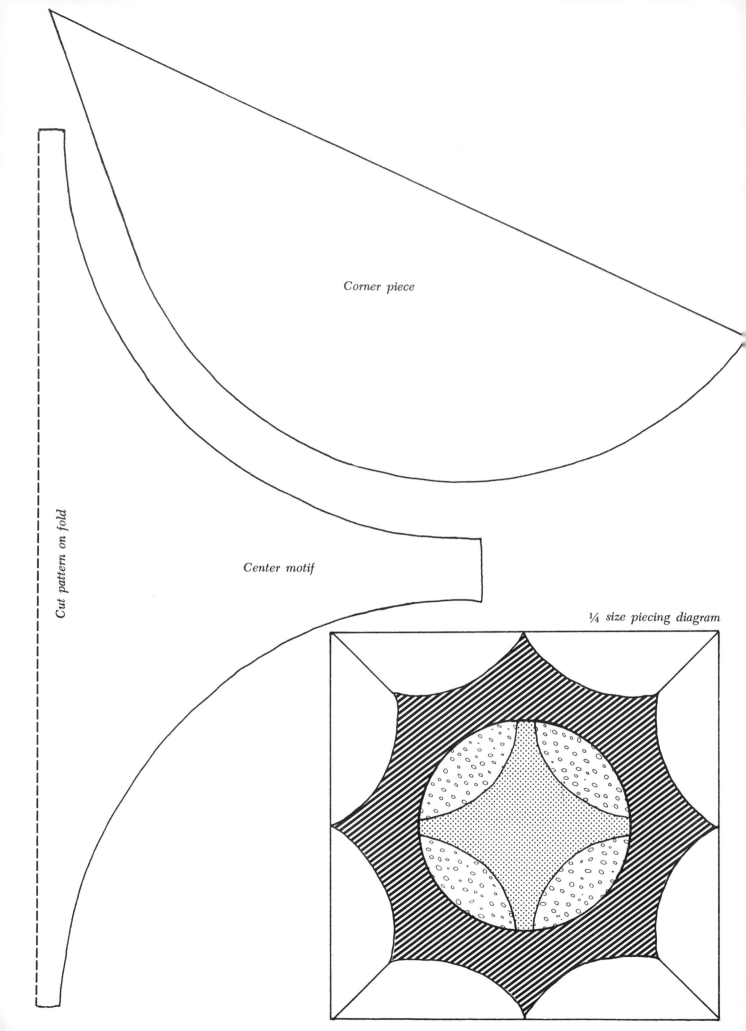

Corner piece

Center motif

Cut pattern on fold

¼ size piecing diagram

Quilting diagram for border (suggested)

Quilting diagram for squares (suggested)

Reverse side of Melon Patch; for right side see the color section.

MELON PATCH   The colors in this design vibrate and shimmer over a hundred years after it was made. There are subtleties of shading created by the use of more than one print in each of the colors and strength in the well-proportioned border. The back, shown in a fold here and in a detail opposite, is a fine example of the decorative effect of the quilting which echoes the shape of the pieces on the top. This quilt is a part of the textile collection at the Kemerer Museum in Bethlehem, and is shown in one of the upstairs rooms in that house. The pattern, two pieces only, is on p. 114.

¼ size piecing diagram

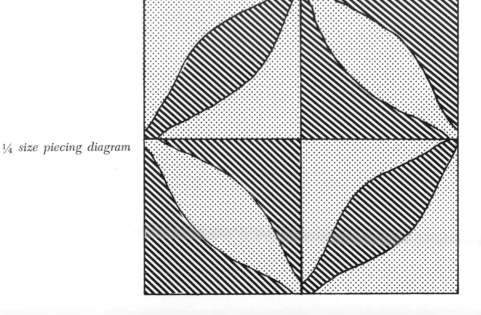

MELON PATCH *The quilt is pieced, with slight curves, suitable for most beginners who are accustomed to handling fabric. The effect is produced by the reversal of colors in alternating squares as in all Robbing Peter to Pay Paul types. Make four squares and join them, then four more, etc.*

The borders are, in order outward from the center, a Saw Tooth 3″ wide, a dark green 4″ wide, a red 3½″ wide and another dark green 3½″ wide. The backing is of a red print.

Quilting is done in echoing lines around each piece. The border is quilted in large zigzag lines.

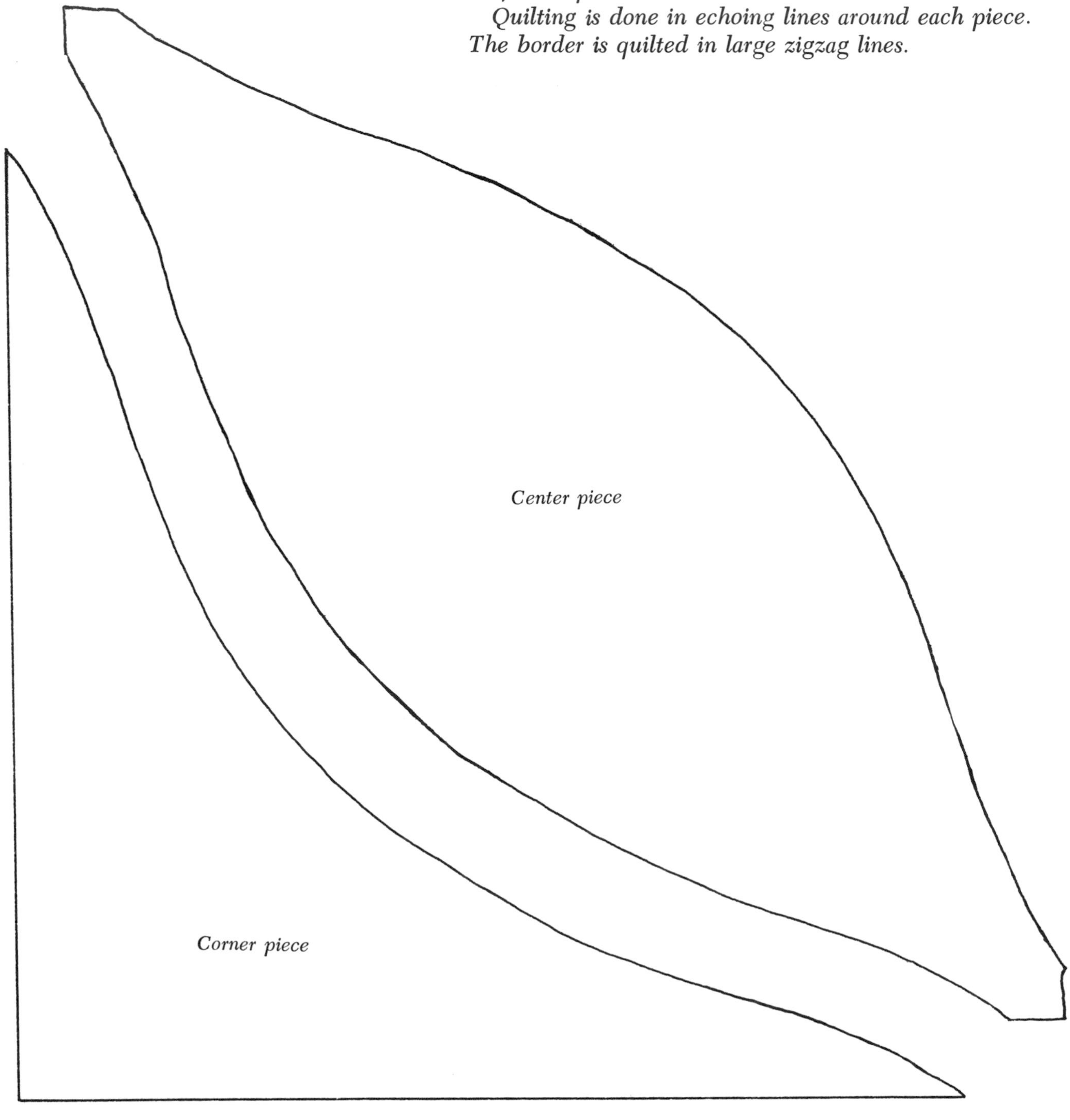

Center piece

Corner piece

TROXELL-STECKEL HOUSE AND FARM MUSEUM

In 1755–56 Peter Troxell, who came from Switzerland, built this fine two-family house for himself and his newly married son. The house and its 410 acres of land were sold to Peter Steckel in 1768 and remained in that family for over 100 years. One Steckel married a Troxell so that for the last years descendants of both families lived there. It was sold out of the family and remained out until Abram P. Steckel bought it in 1942 and presented it to the Lehigh County Historical Society.

The site now contains 17 acres and a typical Pennsylvania barn as well as the stone house which is considered an excellent example of German medieval architecture. One delightful feature is the German inscription over the door which translates to, "God protect this house from all danger. Lead our souls to Heaven." The whitewashed walls and the huge fireplaces make the interior homey and attractive. Located in the small town of Egypt, near Allentown, the museum is open to the public on a limited schedule.

PUSS IN THE CORNER The nine patch division of a quilt square permits infinite variety by further division of each square. The use of color also plays a roll in the final effect. If the corner triangle of Puss in the Corner is white, instead of dark, it is hardly recognizable as the same pattern as the one shown here. The open white center makes it a perfect friendship design; this one is signed in every square. The colors, appropriate for the pastel downstairs bedroom of the Troxell-Steckel Museum, are red and green, the choice for so many Pennsylvania quilts. The proportions and white work and binding make this an example of the art of quilt-making worth studying. The pattern is on p. 117.

PUSS IN THE CORNER *The entire quilt is pieced, all straight lines, suitable for beginners.*

There are four squares across and five squares up and down. Each square is 12″ across. The white connecting borders are 4½″ wide and the white outer border is 7½″ wide. The Saw Tooth border is 2½″ wide.

Quilting is done diagonally across the squares and around all pieces. The borders are quilted with a diamond design and a wave.

Corner squares

Rectangles to form side squares

Center square

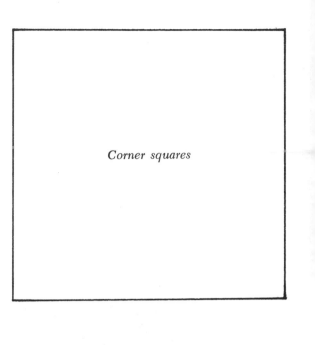

¼ size piecing diagram

Corner triangles

COCKSCOMB   There is no absolute guarantee that the maker of this quilt meant it to be a Cockscomb and not a Thistle, though the strong red and green might give some indication. Both were used as quilt designs in the nineteenth century and both grew in profusion around most farmhouses. There is no doubt about the date of this one because the maker embroidered 1864 and her initials, A.M.K., neatly in the corner. The finely built stone Troxell-Steckel Farm Museum has the clean-swept look that so perfectly suits these Pennsylvania German quilts. They do not belong in the softly gracious rooms of the South or the tiny under-the-eaves rooms of a New England salt box. The less furniture there is in a room, the happier it will be with a Pennsylvania German floral design. The pattern is on pp. 119–121.

COCKSCOMB   *Each square is 22″ and there are 9 in all.*
The border is 11″ wide. The designs are appliquéd.

The quilting in the white areas is in rather random
graceful leaf designs. There is quilting around each
design.

Center motif

¼ size piecing diagram

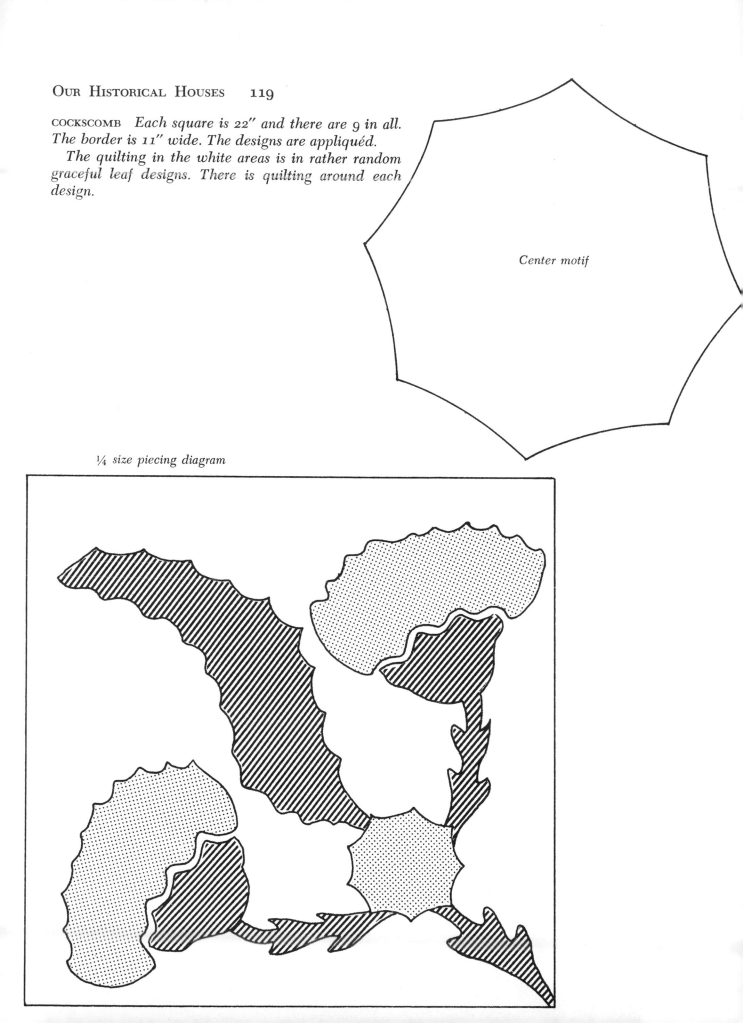

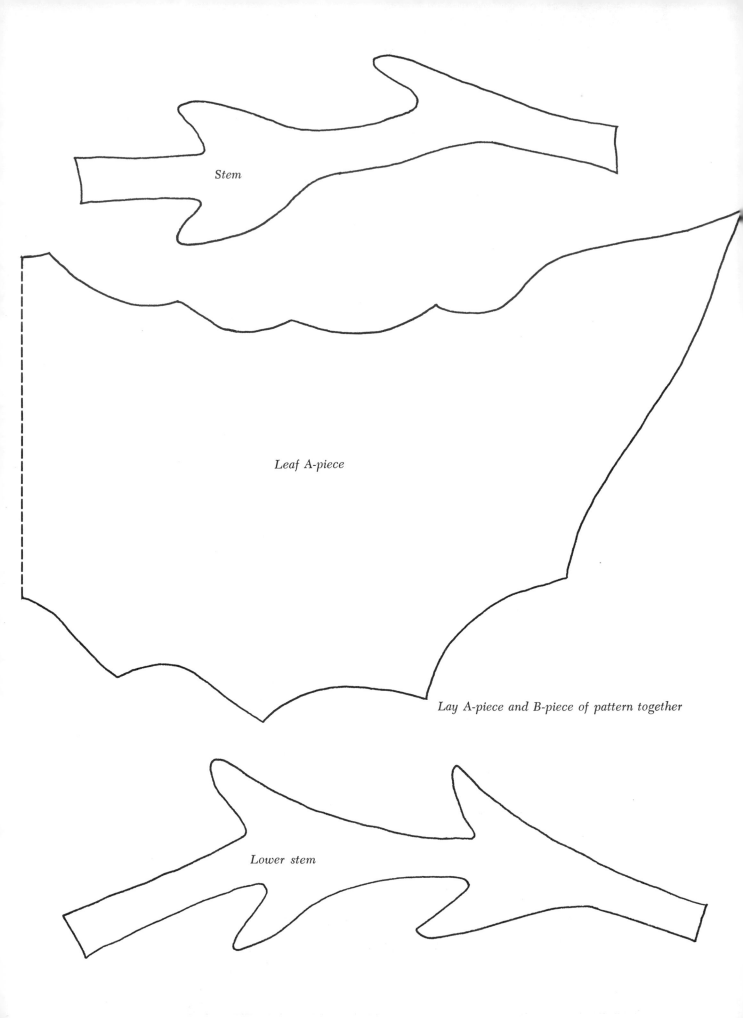

Stem

Leaf A-piece

Lay A-piece and B-piece of pattern together

Lower stem

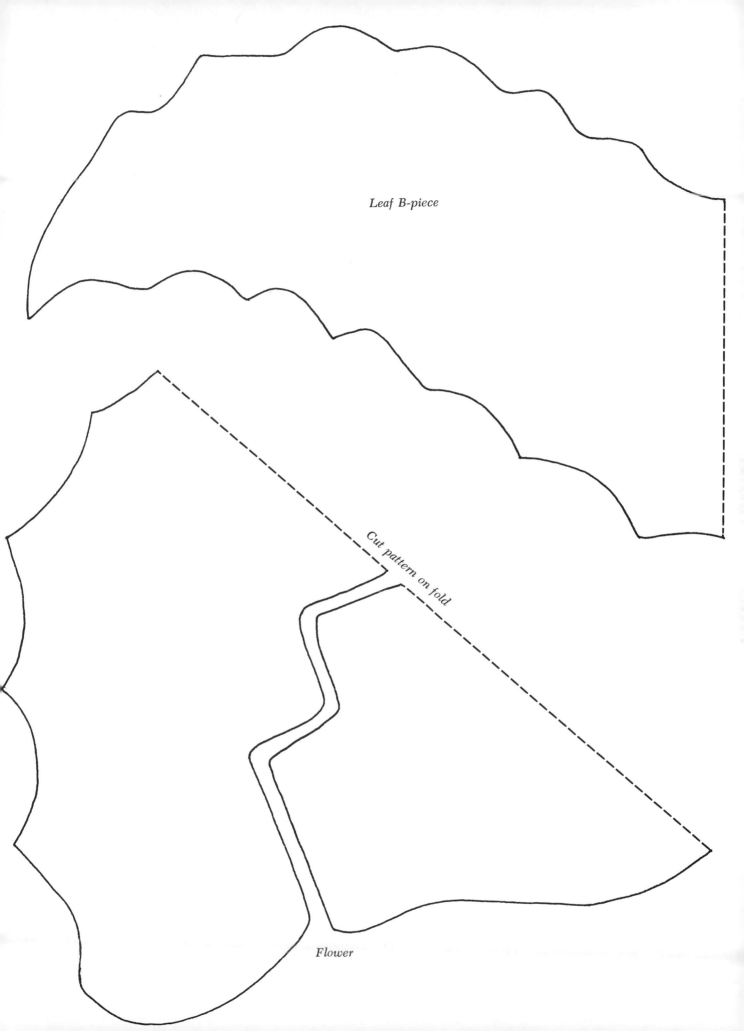

Leaf B-piece

Cut pattern on fold

Flower

MORAVIAN GEMEIN HAUS IN BETHLEHEM

The Gemein Haus or Community House in Bethlehem, Pennsylvania, is now a museum but was once, among other things, the first place of worship for Moravians in America. The lines of the building and the proportions of the rooms are as functional and beautiful today as they were when it was built in the 18th century. The Moravian community was tightly knit and their architecture and crafts were kept to a uniformly high standard wherever they settled in the new world. The sturdy buildings, at first of log and later of brick or stone, with their clean white walls and corner fireplaces, have a uniformly cheerful, neat appearance.

This particular building is part of a still thriving Moravian community which is responsible for a great deal of the charm of Bethlehem where tourists flock, especially at Christmas and Easter. The Moravian Central Church has led the way in preserving many of the handsome buildings in the town which was a prosperous industrial center even before the name, Bethlehem, became synonymous with steel. The Moravian tours are a large part of the holiday festivities today and many of the buildings are open on a year-round basis. Education was always an important part of Moravian life and their schools and colleges still flourish.

TULIP AND WANDERING FOOT   Folk art is apt to accumulate folk tales. One persistent one is that any child who slept under a Wandering Foot quilt would leave home early and roam the earth. Perhaps that is why the name of that design was later changed to Turkey Tracks. Perhaps it is why this inventive nineteenth century quilter interspersed the wandering feet with such homey, inviting tulips. Her design also has a square center where it is usually slightly curved and the border is scalloped and finely bound in red as though she had her own ideas about how her quilts should look. It is in the collection of the Gemein House in Bethlehem. Diagrams and instructions are on pp. 124 & 125.

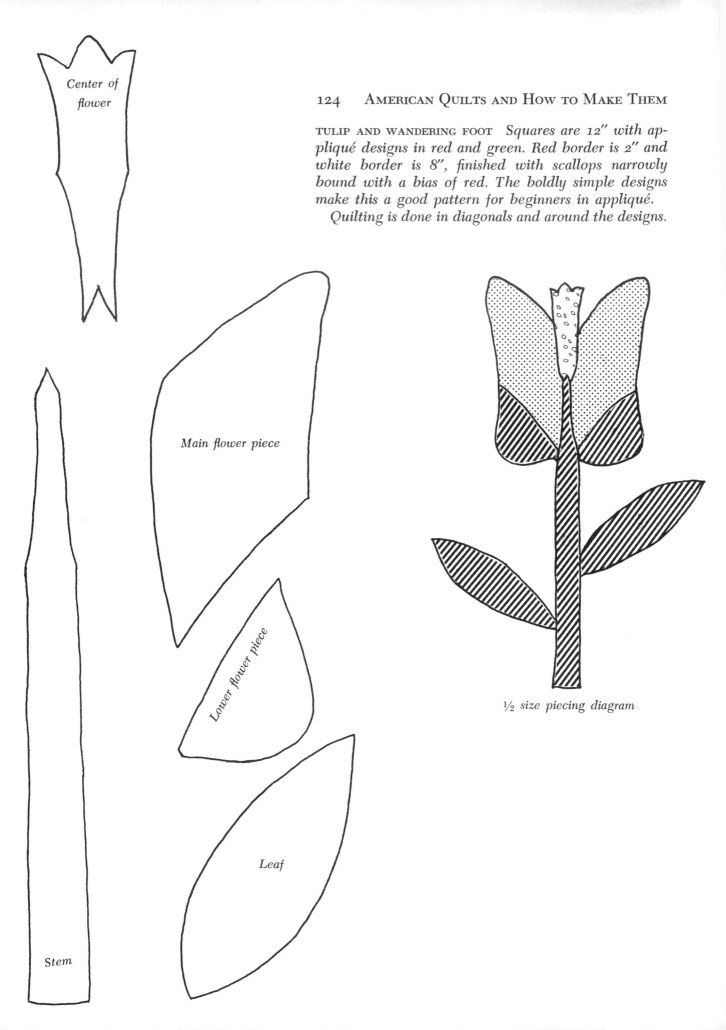

Center of flower

TULIP AND WANDERING FOOT *Squares are 12″ with appliqué designs in red and green. Red border is 2″ and white border is 8″, finished with scallops narrowly bound with a bias of red. The boldly simple designs make this a good pattern for beginners in appliqué.*

Quilting is done in diagonals and around the designs.

Main flower piece

Lower flower piece

½ size piecing diagram

Leaf

Stem

½ size piecing diagram

Piece A

Piece B

ENOCH PRATT HOUSE (*KEYSER MEMORIAL*)

Maryland was long a place of fine houses and elegant living so that this splendid Baltimore town house seems the perfect home for the Maryland Historical Society. It was built in 1847 by Enoch Pratt and purchased in 1919 by Mrs. H. Irvine Keyser for the Society. There are now large modern museum structures adjoining it, but the house is kept as a showplace for fine period furniture, furnishings and costumes. As collections have been donated and more space has been added, this has become a fine city museum, open to the public.

There is a large quilt collection, not on display at all times. Other parts of the very fine textile and costume collections can be seen throughout the buildings. There is also an extensive and fascinating toy collection featuring many dolls and dollhouses. Many students will find this a highly organized and very informative Historical Society.

STAR OF BETHLEHEM These enormous star patterns were much favored by quilters at the turn of the century just after the Revolution. Every good collection boasts at least one. This one in Baltimore's Pratt House seems quite exceptional in its planning and use of color. It was made in 1800 by Dorothy Knight Isaacs but planned and the pieces cut by her husband, Howard Isaacs. The museum calls it a Mathematical Star for very good reason; each point is made up of eight diamond pieces in length and in width, creating a 54″ center square which exactly fits the double bed. The use of floral chintz cut-outs as part of the border design makes this quilt an interesting transitional piece between the appliquéd cut-out ones and the pieced one-patch designs. Working descriptions are on p. 127.

STAR OF BETHLEHEM *Each point of the large star is made up of 64 diamond pieces. The squares and triangles of white that fit into the star to form the 54″ square for the center are 15″ along the star points. There is a plain white 6″ band and then a band made up of 13½″ squares with stars and flowers. The red Saw Tooth design joins the borders and the entire quilt is finished with an 8″ chintz border. The planning of the color is what creates the marvelous kaleidoscope.*

The quilting is done along the lines of the diamonds and in a small diagonal square or diamond in the white part.

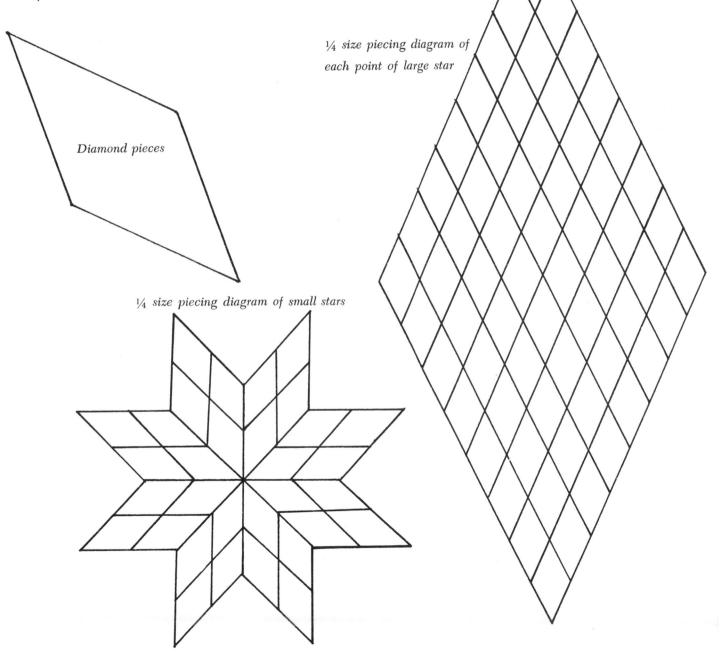

Saw Tooth points

¼ size piecing diagram of each point of large star

Diamond pieces

¼ size piecing diagram of small stars

PATRIOT'S QUILT   The design of this pieced quilt is a rather intricate version of one sometimes called Garden Maze but the truly interesting features of it concern the time of its origin. It was made in Maryland during the Civil War by a lady named Elizabeth Abbe Funk. The fact that she used the Union colors and the small eagle in white work in each octagon shows quite clearly where her sympathies lay. The eagle and stars are said to have been copied from a design in the linoleum in her kitchen. The design is so interlocking that it is hard to say which are the blocks and which are the "sets," if indeed there is any starting and stopping point. The Swag border was very popular in the mid-nineteenth century and makes an interesting balance to the perfect geometry of the main design. Owned by and photographed in The Maryland Historical Society. Patterns are on pp. 129–131.

PATRIOT'S QUILT *The main quilt is pieced and the border appliquéd. It might be wise to handle these pieces more or less continuously, using the paper-backed method described on pp. 40–41.*

Each motif measures almost 8" from the center of the hexagon to the center of the next one so nine by ten motifs will make a 72" x 80" quilt. The borders are 8" wide so that the total 88" x 96" quilt would be suitable for a queen-sized bed.

The centers of the white octagons could be used for signatures or simple white work designs other than the eagle and stars. Look at the Crown design on p. 108 for other suitable quilting diagrams.

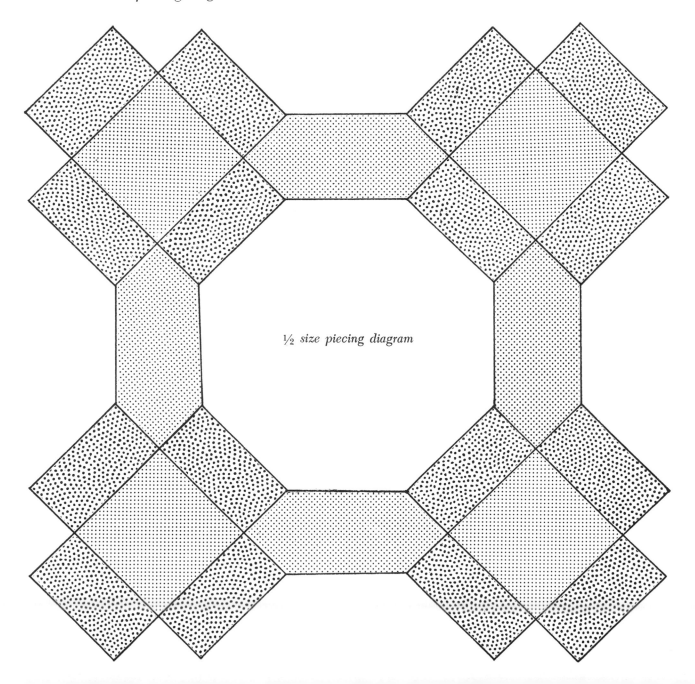

½ *size piecing diagram*

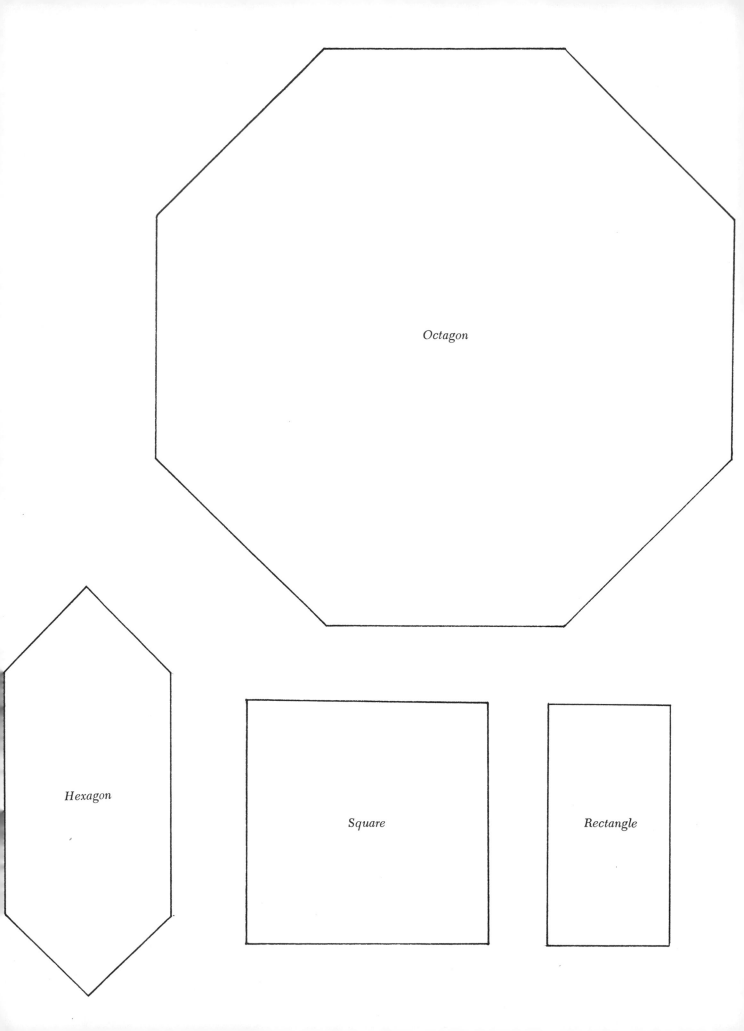

Octagon

Hexagon

Square

Rectangle

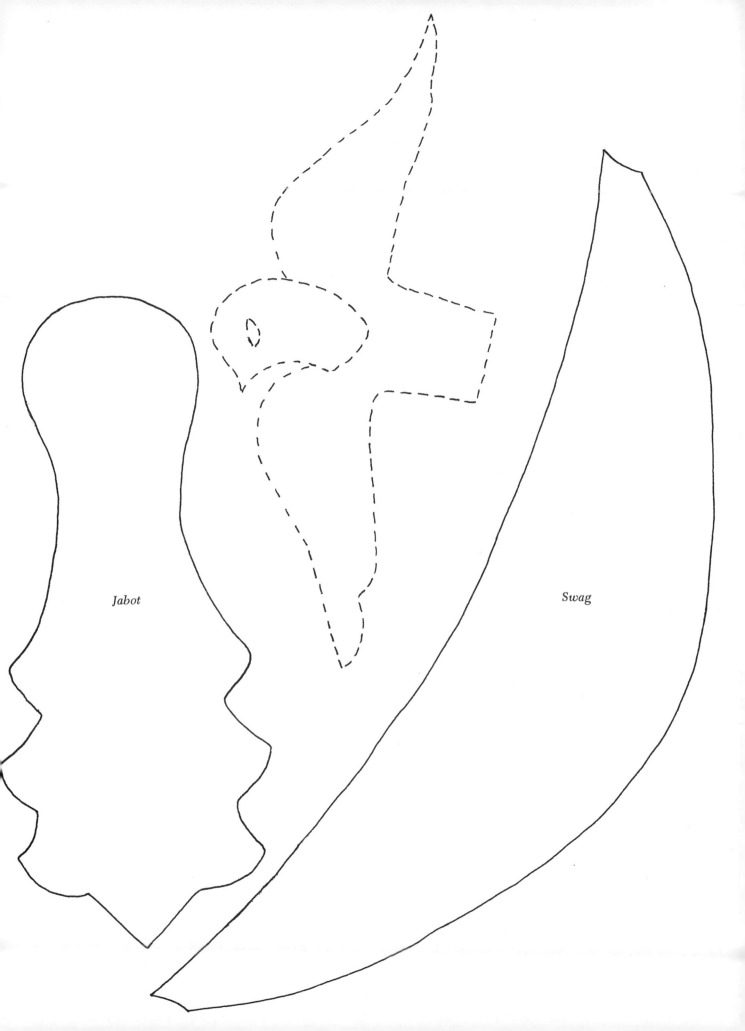

Jabot

Swag

CRIB IRISH CHAIN Mary Emma Bevan was born in 1848 and one of the things that awaited her arrival was this fine Irish Chain quilt. Long years later her daughter gave it to the Maryland Historical Society where it is shown in the Enoch Pratt House. The design is the same as the linsey-woolsey Irish Chain shown on p. 143. The difference is in the fact that the small squares are 1¼″ and the large ones 6¼″ and a third color is introduced into the checkerboard squares, which makes the appearance quite different. The border, made of squares almost ¾″, is identical in style to the border on the large formal Album quilt on pp. 133–134 and color section.

The Formal Baltimore Album quilt in the color section has a variety of beautifully planned squares. These close-ups of seven of the squares are typical of the presentation quilts at their peak in the mid-19th century.

ABRAM'S DELIGHT

Winchester is the gateway to the Shenandoah Valley in Virginia and is a fine historical town in which to stop and spend some time. There are many interesting buildings and for military buffs there are headquarters from both the Revolution and the Civil War. Tucked away in an obscure spot on the edge of town stand two houses worth searching out. One is Abram's Delight, a gracious stone house built in 1754 by Isaac Hollingsworth and lived in continuously until 1930 by the Hollingsworth family. It was purchased by the city in 1943 and turned over to the Winchester Historical Society for restoration.

On the same piece of land is a reproduction of a log cabin of the type built by Abraham Hollingsworth, father of Isaac, when he came to the area in the early eighteenth century. The two houses and their furnishings make a complete picture of the family life of those people who first came over to the valley and settled, and in many cases are still there.

BABY'S ALBUM QUILT   Even the baby had an Album quilt, made for a shower, or by the mother? This late nineteenth century example belongs in a private collection but is shown at Abram's Delight, a house of the type it might have been in. Though it has some of the same cut-paper designs of the larger quilts, it has many designs delicately wrought with strips of bias, very suitable to its small scale.

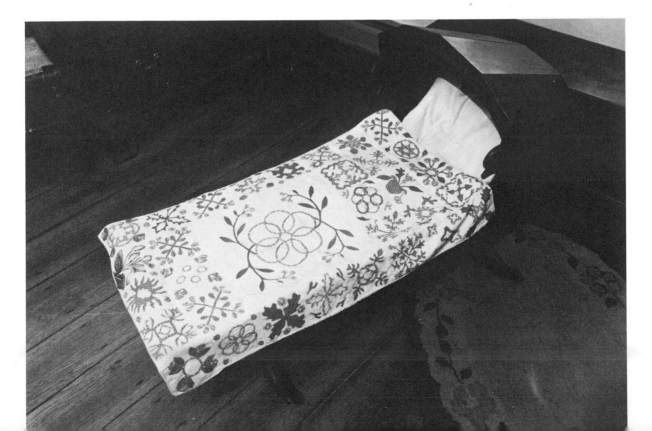

STRATFORD HALL PLANTATION

Thomas Lee, grandson of Richard Lee, the founding father of one of the country's most illustrious families, built Stratford Hall between 1725–30. He is described as a self-educated man but he rose to be President of the King's Council and fathered two men, the only brothers to sign the Declaration of Independence. His great-nephew was "Light Horse Harry" Lee, whose son, Robert E. Lee, was born at Stratford. The house is as interesting as the family, in that it is a style of architecture seen nowhere else in America. The living quarters are on the second floor, in the manner of an Italian Palladian house, It is H-shaped with a marvelous Great Hall in the center, from which one can look across the fields to the Potomac River.

Stratford was purchased in 1929 by the Robert E. Lee Memorial Foundation and opened in 1932. The farm and the mill still operate, the house is a true joy for lovers of furniture and textiles, and the grounds are beautiful at every season of the year.

STRATFORD BEAUTY   The woman who designed and appliquéd this quilt in the late-nineteenth century didn't sign it and didn't give it a name. We kept referring to it as the Stratford Beauty because it is now in the collection of Stratford Hall and it is undoubtedly a beauty, created with a fine eye for design and the most delicate handwork. Though the designs are cut from printed cotton fabric, they are not cut-outs of the print pattern. Each leaf and flower and bird was designed by the maker and the fabric only serves to enhance and soften the effect. Many of the designs are given on pp. 138–141 for you to use in an arrangement of your own or a copy of the original.

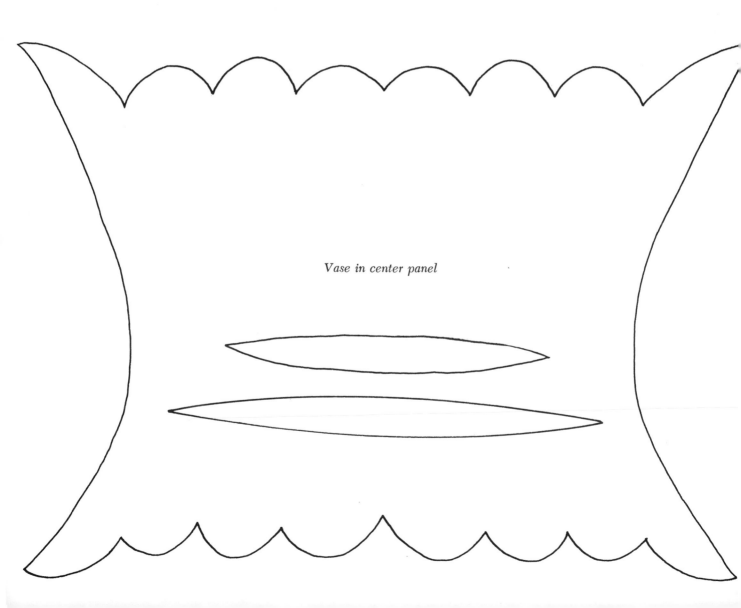

Tulip in center panel

STRATFORD BEAUTY *The center panel is 28″ square. There are five bands around it, starting with a 5″ one, then a 7″ and then three 10″ ones. Each of these is edged with a wave design made of 6½″ x ½″ bias pieces, curved and overlapped.*

The appliqué is all stitched with a very fine close buttonhole stitch. The quilting is done around the designs and in an all-over pattern of the finest possible stitches.

The quality of the handwork signifies a Masterpiece Quilt. It is hardly possible that anyone now would wish to be quite so elaborate or to create a quilt 112″ square, but the general idea and designs could be used for a smaller and simpler production.

Vase in center panel

Plume in border #3

Oak leaf in border #4

Small leaves

Petal in groups in border #1 and #2

Rosettes for border #1

Grape leaf for center panel and border #3

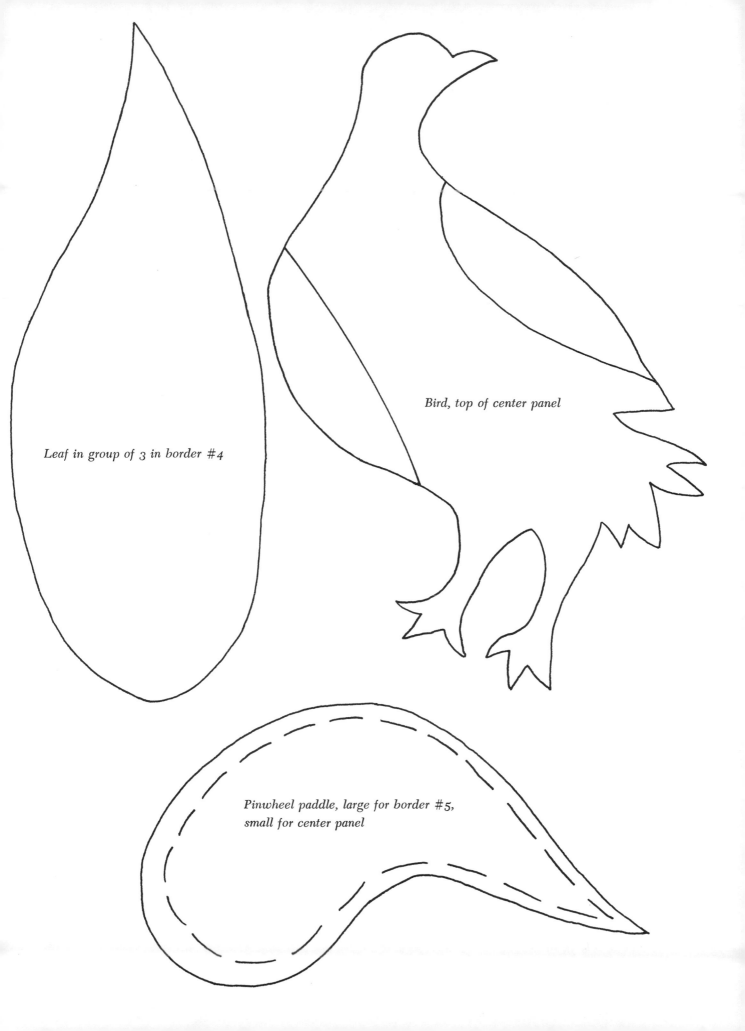

Leaf in group of 3 in border #4

Bird, top of center panel

Pinwheel paddle, large for border #5,
small for center panel

GUNSTON HALL PLANTATION

Just down the Potomac River from Mt. Vernon a Virginia gentleman known as "The Pen of the Revolution," George Mason, built an especially fine square brick house. He started it in 1755 and then turned the job over to an English architect named William Buckland whose taste in interiors was exquisite. In matters of his budding country George Mason stood as solidly as his house. He wrote the Virginia Declaration of Rights which was the basis of the Federal Bill of Rights and he refused to sign the Constitution because it did not provide for the abolition of slavery, nor did it safeguard, as he thought it should, the rights of any individual. Mason died in 1792 but his house and his ideas still stand.

Mr. and Mrs. Louis Hertle bought Gunston Hall in 1912 and left it to the Commonwealth of Virginia. During the last twenty years it has been restored and the magnificent boxwood gardens tended and some of the original furnishings returned. It is open every day except Christmas.

IRISH CHAIN IN LINSEY-WOOLSEY We're proud to have this early quilt in our collection, dating from 1750 and in marvelous condition! Several people who have seen the quilt on the schoolmaster's bed at Gunston Hall have insisted that it is a woven coverlet because it is of linsey-woolsey, but it is a true piece-work quilt. It is also notable because it has the cut-out bottom corners to fit around the bed posts, a feature which seemed to disappear about 1800, in spite of its great practicality. For this photograph the quilt was moved into the big house from the school house and shown on a bed in one of the small upstairs children's rooms. Diagrams are on p. 144.

IRISH CHAIN   *In spite of the complex appearance of this design, it is essentially alternating plain and checkerboard squares. In this case the large plain square is 14″ each way and the optical illusion is created by piecing one of the small red squares into each corner of it. The checkerboard is then made of thirteen blue and twelve red squares, as shown.*

⅙ size piecing diagram

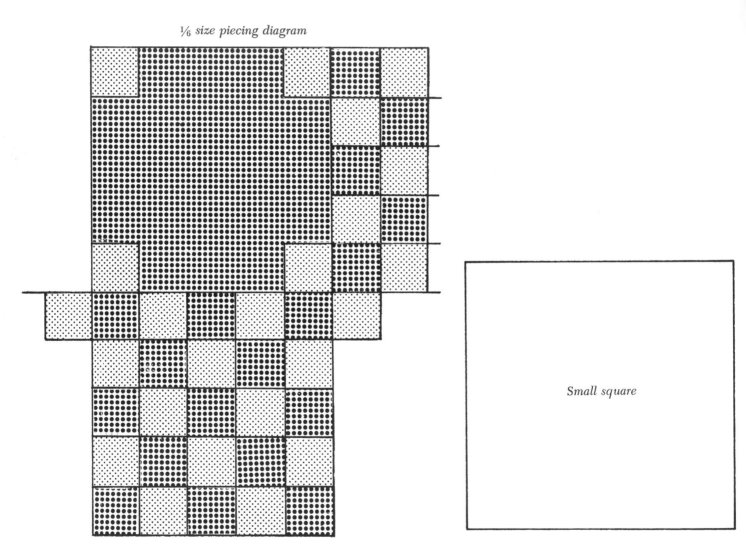

Small square

WREATH AND HEARTS There was a time when all young ladies were taught needlework from earliest childhood. They made samplers and quilts and all manner of fine pieces for their hope chests. In some parts of the country a girl was not considered ready to marry until she had made her baker's dozen quilts, the last one being the finest, her bridal quilt. The delicacy of this wreath design and the addition of the little hearts make it possible that it is such a bridal quilt. It was made in the early nineteenth century and is now at Gunston Hall, not on display, though it is quite in keeping with the architecture. The dark pink and green, softened by so much white, is entirely different in overall effect from the Pennsylvania German quilts in the same colors. Designs on pp. 146 & 147.

WREATH AND HEARTS   *The squares are 12¾″ with appliqué design. There are four squares across and six lengthwise. The border, 12¾″ wide, goes around only three sides. The vines and circles are made from bias strips of fabric, finished ½″ wide.*

Quilting is done around the appliqué and as a repeat of the leaves in any open white spaces.

½ size piecing diagram of square

½ size piecing diagram of border

BELLE GROVE

In 1794 Major Isaac Hite, brother in law of James Madison, sent his architect to Thomas Jefferson of Monticello to ask his advice on building a house. The house, on a 483 acre tract of land in the Shenandoah Valley near Middletown, Va., was built shortly thereafter and named Belle Grove. It is a one-story stone house of elegant proportions with high ceilinged rooms and magnificent views. Major Hite eventually had 7,437 acres of land around the house and twelve children in it. It remained in the Hite family until 1860.

The last owner of Belle Grove, Francis Hunnewell, bequeathed it and 100 acres of land to the National Trust for Historic Preservation. It is today a lively place full of cultural activities, classes, demonstrations and information.

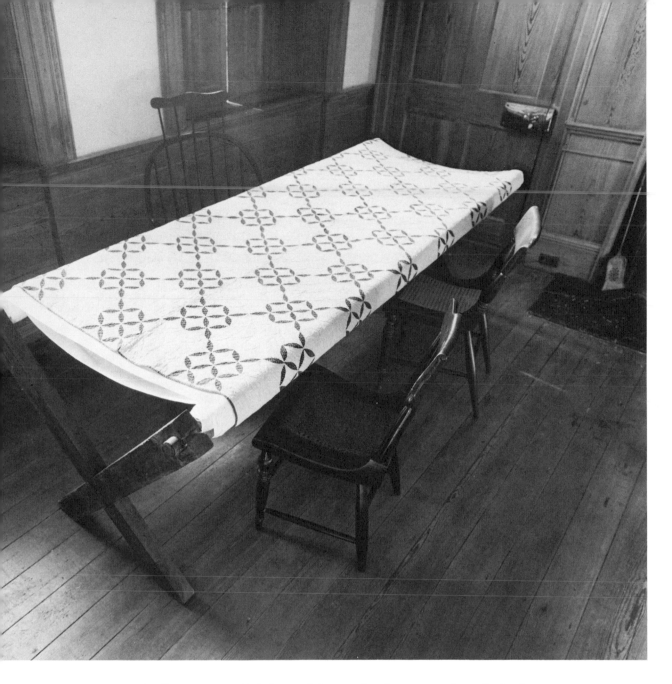

ORANGE PEEL A charming and delicate blue and white pieced quilt is shown here on the frame at Belle Grove. It was made in the early 19th century by Sarah Branson LeHew and her daughter-in-law, Sally Manchin Hopewell Le-Hew. The fine curved piecing and the quilting, which exactly echoes the pieced design, are typical of the quality of work by these talented needlewomen. Three of their quilts are still in existence and they all have handwoven cotton backs, which are believed to have been made by the LeHew women. The place of origin of this quilt is Lost River, one of those towns which was in Virginia until the Civil War when West Virginia became a state. It is now in a fine private textile collection in Nineveh in the Shenandoah Valley. Many of the pieces from this collection are seen at Belle Grove on loan. Design on p. 150.

ORANGE PEEL   *Each square is made up of four squares, which in turn are pieced of four each of the two shapes given. The whole square is 7″ as are the white intervening squares. By using only piece no. 1 the designs can be appliquéd onto 3½″ white squares.*

The quilting is done around the orange peel design and echoes it in the plain white squares.

½ *size piecing diagram*

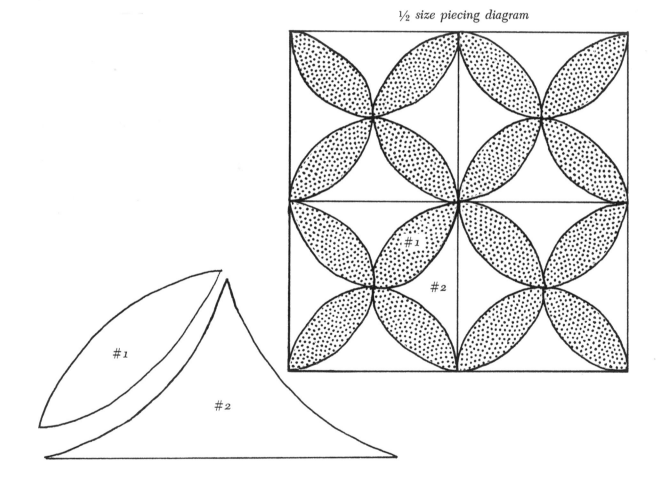

INDIAN TRAILS AND VARIABLE STAR   Photographed at Belle Grove, where it is part of the National Trust collection, this quilt makes use of two designs in dark earth tones. The browns were probably more uniform in shade at one time but some have faded more than others, whereas the red and dark green are still vibrant. The browns were undoubtedly scrapbag pieces and the thread is said to be re-used as it is of several varieties and colors. Such frugality was not unusual in frontier or backwoods communities where everything was hard to come by. The quilt was made by the Gillian family of Illinois, which in the early and mid-nineteenth century was pretty far west.

The large design can also be called Kansas Troubles or Irish Puzzle, and the small design, with slight variations, can be called Lone Star and many other Stars. The four squares of the large design are often rearranged and called by other names, such as Barrister's Block and Rocky Glen. Designs on pp. 152 & 153.

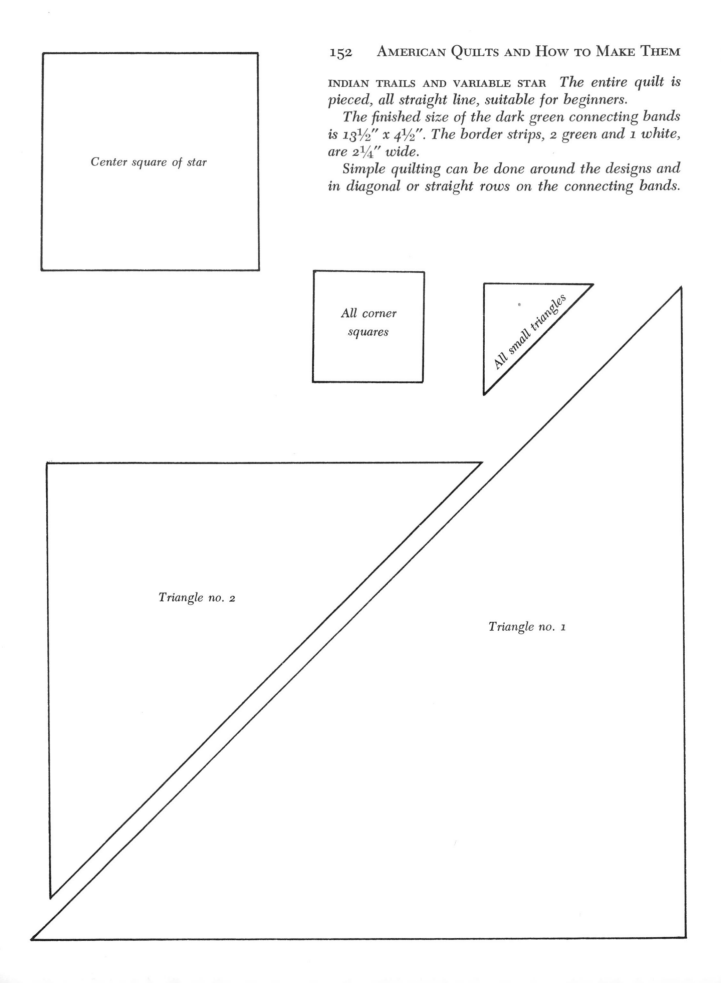

Center square of star

INDIAN TRAILS AND VARIABLE STAR   *The entire quilt is pieced, all straight line, suitable for beginners.*

The finished size of the dark green connecting bands is 13½″ x 4½″. The border strips, 2 green and 1 white, are 2¼″ wide.

Simple quilting can be done around the designs and in diagonal or straight rows on the connecting bands.

All corner squares

All small triangles

Triangle no. 2

Triangle no. 1

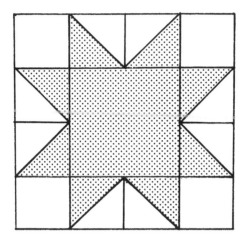

½ size piecing diagram

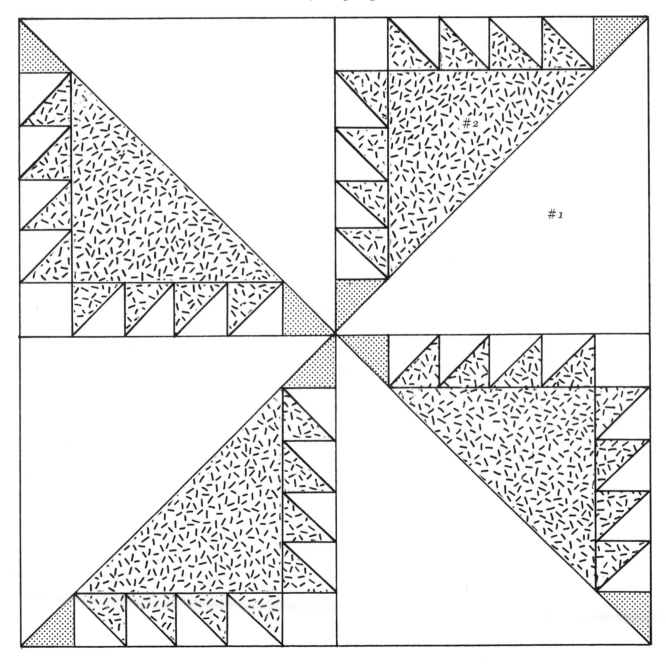

CHERRY TREES   The great delicacy of this 1856 quilt makes it perfect for a bride or for any young girl. It was made by M. S. Baker, of the same family as the T. A. Baker Tulip on p. 156. The white work is intricate and superb and the appliqué is stitched so finely that the stitches are hardly visible. This family was one of those that must have been celebrated for its talented needlewomen. The descendants are fortunate in still owning these quilts. The photograph was made at Belle Grove where the quilts were on loan. For pattern suggestions see p. 155.

CHERRY TREES   *The trees are partly appliquéd and partly worked in the quilting on 13″ squares. Stems and trunks are double rows of quilting connecting the green leaves and red cherries.*

The border is 11″ wide with a long strip of ½″ bias dividing the right-side-up small trees from the upside-down ones. There are a few extra leaves in between to add color.

The alternating white work squares are finely worked in varying designs. Another possibility would be to work an all-white repeat of the tree squares.

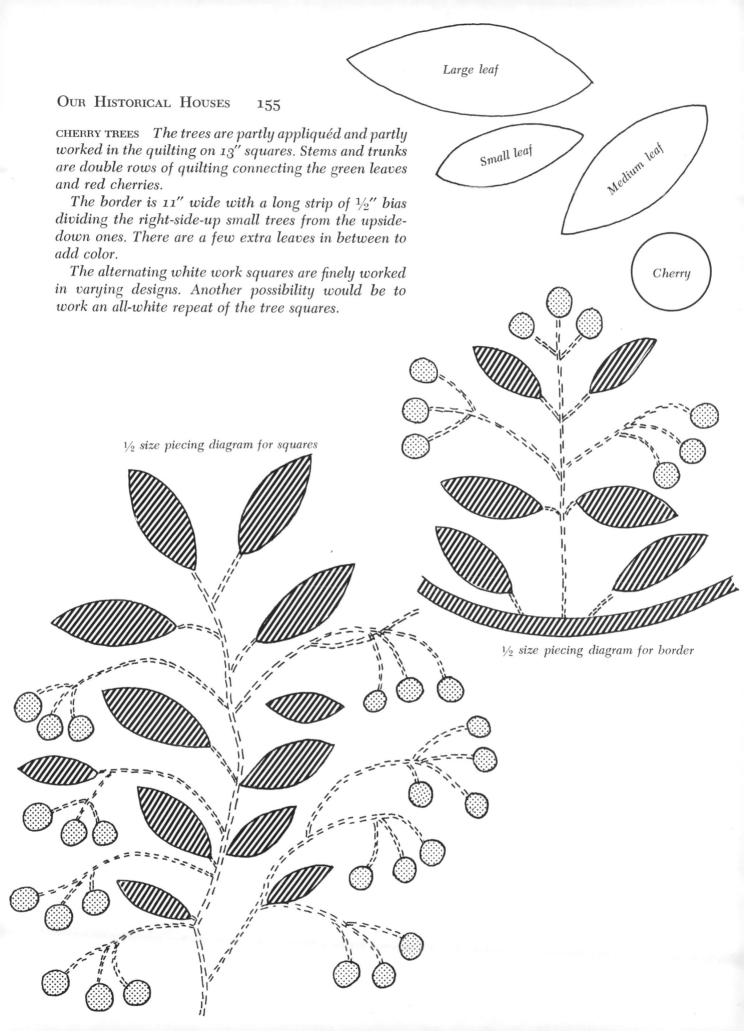

Large leaf

Small leaf

Medium leaf

Cherry

½ size piecing diagram for squares

½ size piecing diagram for border

TULIP   T. A. Baker appliquéd and quilted this colorful work of art in the year 1865, shortly before she married George W. Miley, a Confederate soldier. He was imprisoned in the North and she must have put all her energies into the preparations for her marriage, embellishing every inch of her quilts with intricate white work. The colors seem bold and young and the choice of a cheerful flower design with a Fruitful Vine border says something of the optimistic nature of the designer. Her granddaughter still owns this quilt, which was photographed in Belle Grove, where it was on loan for an exhibit. Partial patterns for use in your own version are on p. 157.

TULIP *The entire quilt is appliquéd, each large motif on a 34" square. The border is 11" wide with a Fruitful Vine motif of leaves and stuffed grapes. The same leaf patterns can be used for both the Tulip squares and the border. The grape pattern is also used for the small round designs on the large squares all of which are padded. All vines and stems are made of bias strips about ⅝" finished width.*

The very fine quilting varies and is based on common garden flowers. From a collector's standpoint the name and date worked with such clarity is an added bonus.

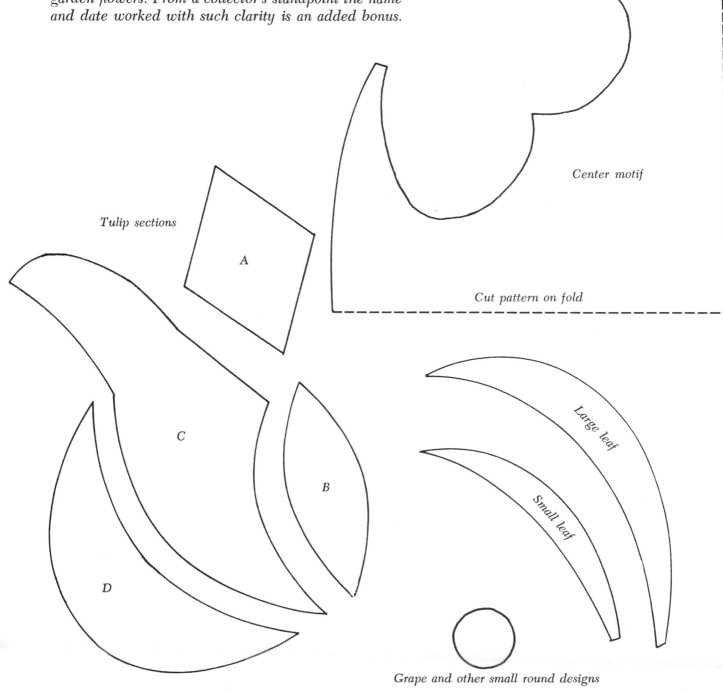

Center motif

Cut pattern on fold

Tulip sections

A

C

B

D

Large leaf

Small leaf

Grape and other small round designs

SULLY PLANTATION HOUSE

Richard Bland Lee, Northern Virginia's first Congressman, built a handsome three-story frame house in 1794 in Fairfax County, Virginia. The land was a grant of 3111 acres from Lord Fairfax to the Lee family in 1725, when it was still rather wild country by the standards of the people who had built the great plantation houses in tidewater.

Though the barn was destroyed by fire, the house was fortunate in always having loving and protective owners over the years. In 1958 it was slated for demolition due to the building of Dulles Airport, which called for the use of that acreage remaining with the house.

Legislation instigated by Eleanor Lee Templeman, a great great granddaughter of Richard Bland Lee, saved the home from destruction. It was then turned over to the Fairfax County Park Authority to maintain for the public. Happily, though the jets from Dulles fly directly overhead, much of the 18th century serenity is preserved here.

SUNBURST The geometric simplicity of this design made it an early favorite and it seems to have acquired a large variety of names. Mariner's Compass, Sunflower, and Rolling Pin Wheel are only a few of the many versions. The design can be pieced or appliquéd and there are those who say that when it is pieced it is a Mariner's Compass and when it is appliquéd, it is called by one of the other names. It seems more likely that what was a Mariner's Compass in Boston became a Sunflower in Kansas. It is often made as a scrap quilt but this one fits the more formal atmosphere of Sully because of its use of one solid color on white and the very even arrangement of the designs and the Saw Tooth border. It was made before 1850 and is in the collection of the house. For working diagram see pp. 160–161.

SUNBURST *The design can be appliquéd onto a 15″ white square or pieced into a circle and then joined to the square. For appliqué cut the center circle and 12 pieces each of no. 1 and no. 2, all in the chosen color. For piecing the full circle, cut those same pieces in the chosen color plus 12 each of no. 3 and no. 4 and 24 of no. 5, all in white.*

The Sully quilt is almost square, with 6 blocks in each direction plus a 10″ border on three sides. The Sunburst is slightly over 11″ in diameter so that you could reduce the size of the quilt by using 12″ blocks. You can also change the dimensions by using less blocks across and the same or more lengthwise.

Quilting is done around the circles and in diagonal 1″ squares over the rest of the surface.

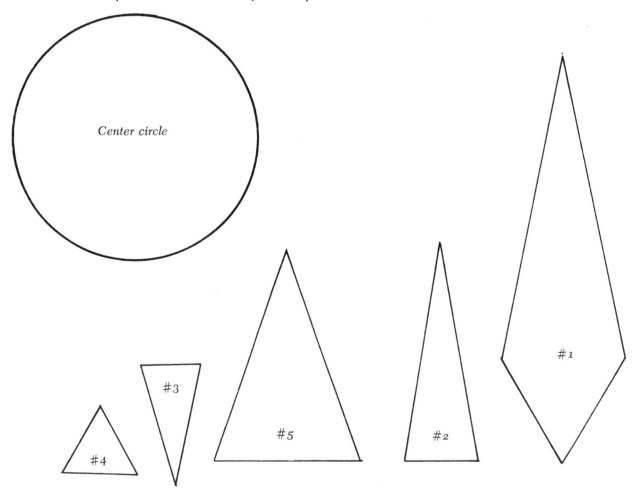

Center circle

#3

#4

#5

#2

#1

½ size piecing diagram

FLORAL FANTASY   Once in a while a quilter took off on paths unexplored before and achieved elaborate and startling effects. This quilt, probably from the early nineteenth century, is now owned by the Society of the Lees of Virginia and was photographed at a Lee home, Sully. The flowers made of gathered strips are quite unusual, and in combination with the octagonal settings and the scalloped border mark this as a masterpiece quilt. The colors may have been even brighter but the years have taken their toll of dyes and so it is impossible to tell whether the bows, for instance, were always white. There may well have been a paler pink in all the pieces that are now white. For partial patterns and suggestions see pp. 164–166.

Leaf

Leaf

FLORAL FANTASY *The gathered pieces for the round flowers may be cut in either straight or bias strips, the width shown in the patterns and slightly longer than the outer edges. On the large flower this will be about 16" for the longer piece and about 10" for the shorter one. The strip for the small flower will be about 9". (There is one flower which has a narrow strip of yet another color near the center; this seems unnecessary.) Gather the outer edge of the outer strip slightly so that it fits the circle. Appliqué it in place. Gather the inner edge and pin or baste it flat so that the next piece can be appliquéd over it. Test both bias and straight strips in the fabric you have chosen before deciding which you like best.*

¼ size piecing diagram

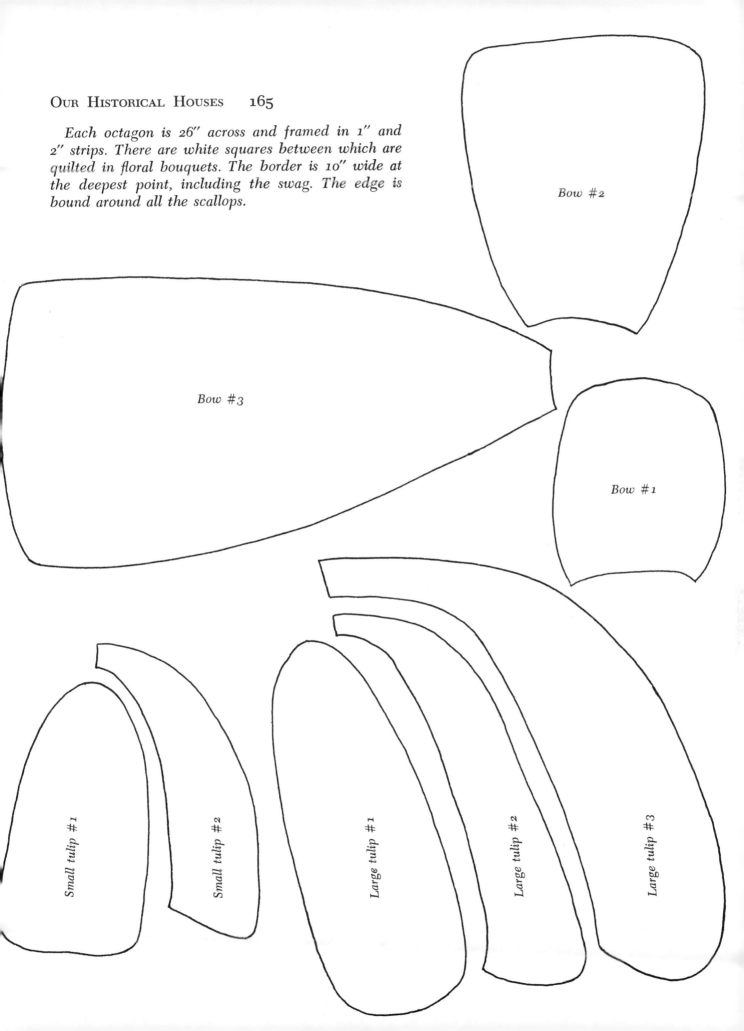

Each octagon is 26″ across and framed in 1″ and 2″ strips. There are white squares between which are quilted in floral bouquets. The border is 10″ wide at the deepest point, including the swag. The edge is bound around all the scallops.

Bow #2

Bow #3

Bow #1

Small tulip #1

Small tulip #2

Large tulip #1

Large tulip #2

Large tulip #3

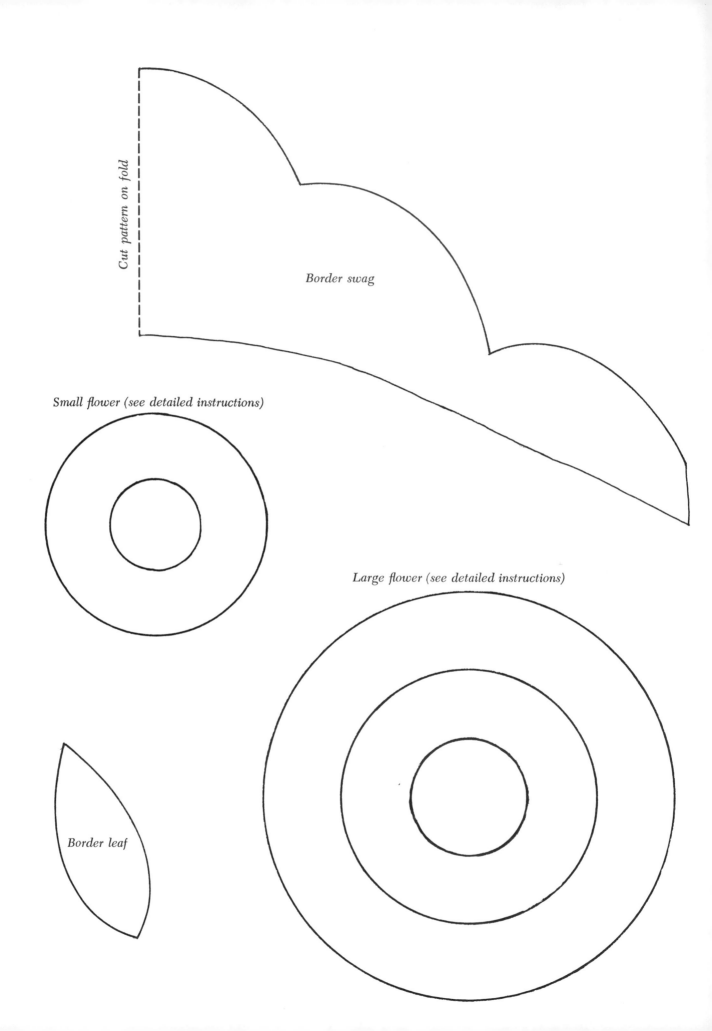

Cut pattern on fold

Border swag

Small flower (see detailed instructions)

Large flower (see detailed instructions)

Border leaf

The lower right section of the Sully Album quilt shows the typical flower baskets and wreaths of the mid-19th century. Notice how many are similar to the ones on pp. 88–90 and pp. 133–134 though the overall effect is quite different from either of the others.

ZEBULON B. VANCE BIRTHPLACE

In the state of North Carolina Zebulon Vance stands out as the ultimate hero. In the best tradition of American heroes, he was born in a log house far up in the mountains, served his country as soldier and politician, always working hard for everything he cherished. The firing on Fort Sumpter changed him from a man who did not believe in the dissolution of the Union to a strong Confederate leader. While on the field of battle as colonel of a regiment, he was elected governor of North Carolina. During his term in office he was captured and imprisoned in Washington, D.C., for seven weeks. After the war, he practiced law and served again as governor and as U.S. Senator.

The log house that stands now is an accurate reconstruction of the original, standing on the same foundation and built around the original massive chimney. There are many of the original timbers and much of the inside woodwork of the first house. It can hardly be called a log cabin because of its size and fine furnishing. There are five generous rooms, of which only the kitchen does not contain a bed. This is the typical mountain style of furnishing with a bed even in the living room; there were in total ten people to bed down in this family! Restoration of outbuildings and museum facilities continues at the site near Weaverville, North Carolina.

OAK LEAF CLUSTER This quilt was signed in 1861 with the name Katherine Varian and the interesting information that she was, at that time, seventy-three years old. How many wonderful quilts she must have made to be able to plan and create one as perfect as this! The design is a sister to the Grapeleaf Reel on p. 163, but look at the intriguing difference in effect gained by the use of a strong red frame and white cross-bars. The decoration of the cross-bars in itself is a delight, the white work designs varying from vines to flowers to hearts, punctuated at the corners with small appliqué designs. The room is an upstairs bedroom at the Vance Birthplace. On p. 169 you will find patterns for the Oak Leaf Cluster.

OAK LEAF CLUSTER *The center of this design can be pieced, as far out as piece #3, then it and the remainder appliquéd to a 13″ white square.*

The red bands are 1½″ wide. They can be made of two 10″ strips and two 16″ strips or mitered at the corners from four 16″ strips. The cross bar "sets" are 2½″ wide with small Orange Peel designs in each intersection.

The quilting is very fine and in the white part very original. Each "set" has different designs of flowers, hearts and leaves.

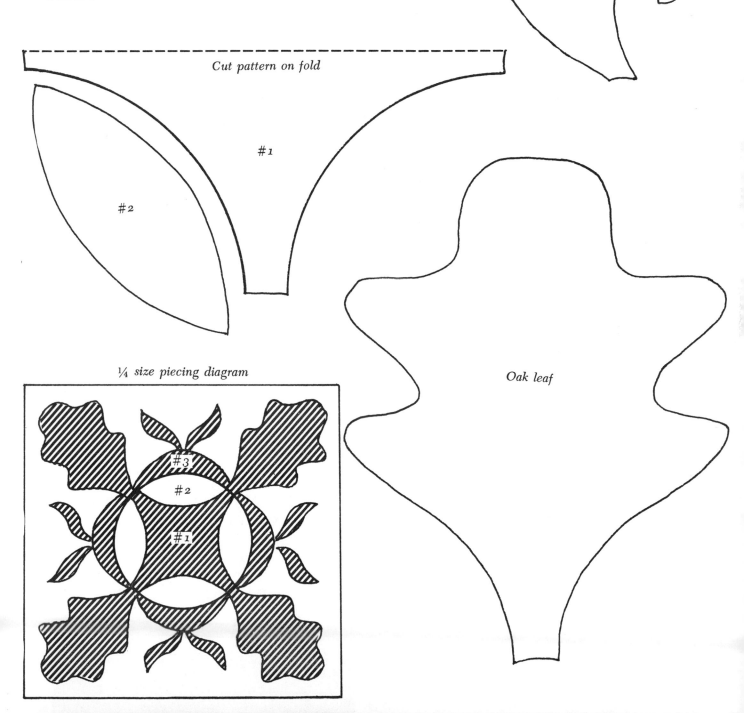

#3

Small leaf

Cut pattern on fold

#1

#2

¼ size piecing diagram

Oak leaf

ROBBING PETER TO PAY PAUL   The intricacy of effect and optical illusion created with simple interlocking circles in two colors never ceases to amaze and stun the beholder of such pieced quilts. In the southern Appalachian region from which this pre-Civil War quilt comes, it was known as Robbing Peter to Pay Paul but is known in other parts of the country as Orange Peel (not to be confused with the one on p. 149) and Dolly Madison's Workbox. Some other designs which have the interchanging color, optical illusion effect, such as Melon Patch on p. 113, are also known as Robbing Peter to Pay Paul designs. The Vance Birthplace is the perfect setting for the navy blue print and white quilt and for the overshot coverlet. The pattern is on p. 171.

ROBBING PETER TO PAY PAUL   *This quilt is pieced in two colors always alternating and without "sets." The design is created from interlocking circles, resulting in two pattern pieces. The curves are easy enough for a skilled beginner to attempt.*

No sets are used and no borders are necessary though bands of two colors would be attractive.

The quilting is all done in echoes of the pattern shapes.

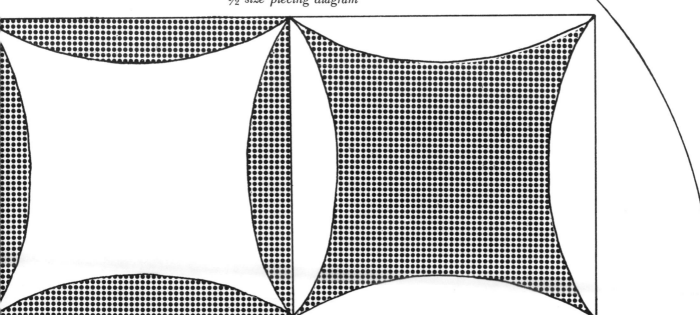

Center piece

Cut pattern on fold

½ size piecing diagram

FEATHERED STAR The green and pink design in the carefully pieced Feathered Star blends with the delicately stitched Sunflower quilting to let us know what a fine needlewoman made this quilt shown in the Vance Birthplace. It is a bit sad that she did not sign or date it but perhaps she felt that anyone who saw it would know who did work of such quality. In many areas it is said that people could tell at a glance who had done which quilt when they were hung side by side at a county fair. To the quiltmakers a neighbor's admiration undoubtedly seemed more important than what anyone might think over 100 years later! The designs are on pp. 173–175.

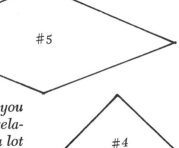

FEATHERED STAR *Look at this design as a true nine-patch, which it is, and you will see that piecing one patch at a time and then three strips will make it relatively easy to handle. Even though it is all straight line piecing, it requires a lot of skill to keep such small pieces in line. It might even be necessary to use the paper-backed method described on pp. 40–41 for the joining of the very small squares and triangles.*

The border is appliquéd, using a finished bias of about 5⁄8″ for the vine. The total width of the border is 7″, finished with a bias binding of the green. The white squares (or diamonds since they are diagonally placed) used to set the 13″ pieced squares together are also 13″.

The quilting is done in a fine symmetrical Sunflower design and in straight and diagonal rows as well as around the pieces of the feathered star.

½ *size piecing diagram*

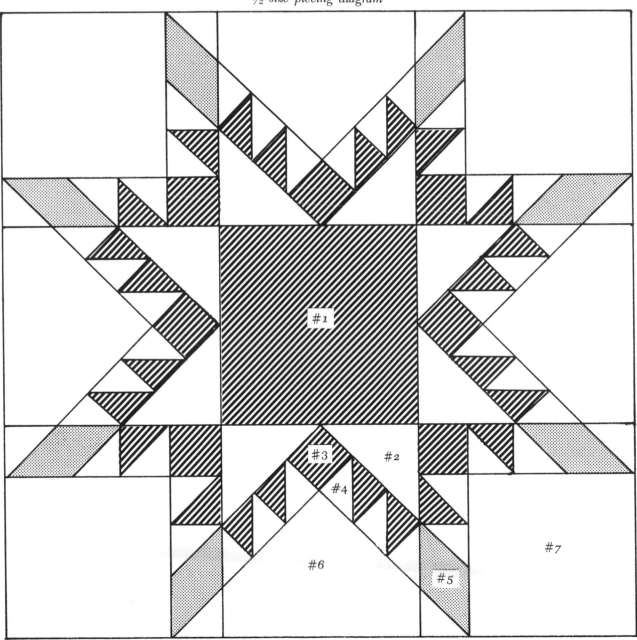

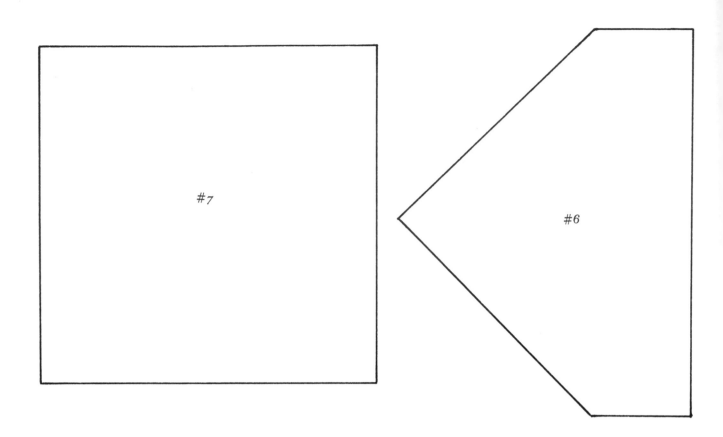

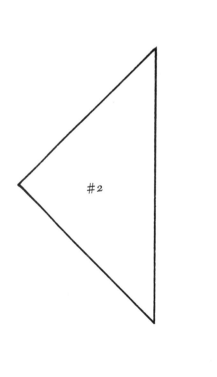

#7

#6

#2

#1

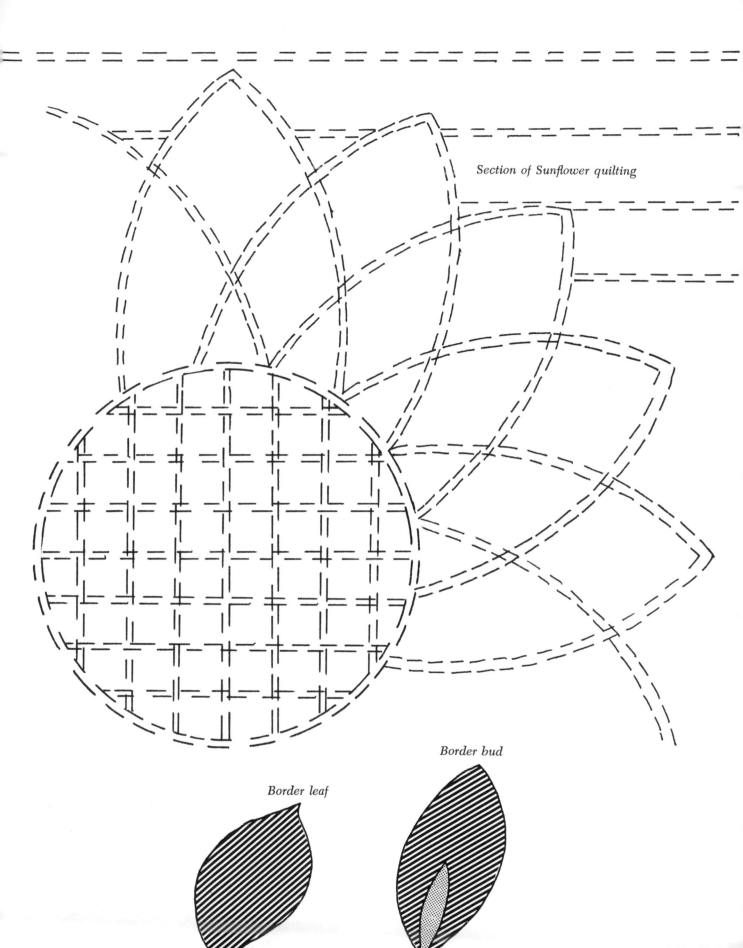

Section of Sunflower quilting

Border bud

Border leaf

OLD SALEM

Museum villages are surely among the most charming ways to look into our past and Old Salem, North Carolina, rates high among them. Salem was settled by Moravians in 1766 and became a thriving community known for its hospitality and fine craftsmanship. It was among the first planned communities in America and certainly one of the most successful. Eventually a non-Moravian town, Winston, grew up just north of it and the two communities merged into Winston-Salem.

Just after World War II it became evident that the beautifully constructed buildings of Salem would be torn down for shopping centers and service stations. Some did meet such a fate but many were saved by Old Salem Incorporated. The restoration still marches on and the village lives again for the visitors who come to enjoy it. The bakery is operating and bread can be purchased there. The Salem Tavern Dining Room provides one of the finest meals any traveler can hope for, in an early American setting. There is an excellent museum, The Museum of Early Southern Decorative Arts, associated with Old Salem, in which those who love furniture and textiles can spend a great deal of time. In planning a trip to Old Salem, one should allow at least an entire day.

DRUNKARD'S PATH   There is possibly no one quilt pattern with more variations than this simple two-patch. Usually, the small patches are set together in groups of sixteen to form a large block, but the trick is in which way those sixteen are turned in relationship to each other. Eight of the sixteen employ a light and dark piece in one arrangement and the other eight in the opposite. The Drunkard's Path is one of the most common arrangements but this one employs a fairly uncommon color combination and employs two dark colors for variation. This quilt came from the Shore or Schor family in Yadkin County, North Carolina, as did the bold T-Block on p. 178, and they certainly show a strong family resemblance. It is shown in the Vogler House at Old Salem, where it is now in residence. The simple pattern is on p. 177.

DRUNKARD'S PATH *The quilt shown is pieced in two colors and white, though one dark color or all dark scrap bag pieces can be used with white. In this case the trick is to run all of one color to make a diagonal line in one direction and the other color so as to make a diagonal line in the other direction.*

The patches should be made as follows: eight with the dark as the larger piece, and eight with the dark as the smaller piece. They are then set edge-to-edge to form one large block. The large blocks are also set edge-to-edge. The border used here is three bands, about 2" wide each of the dark colors.

The quilting can be done around the pieces only or in echoes of the outline.

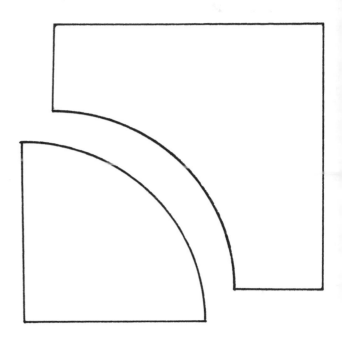

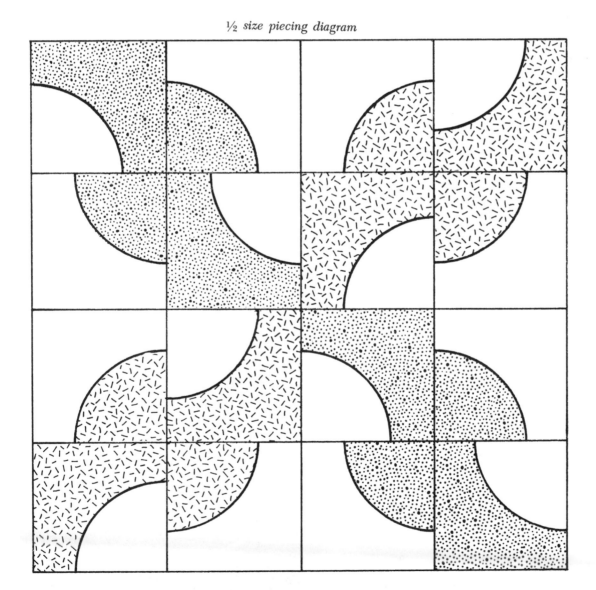

½ size piecing diagram

CAESAR'S CROWN   Well-planned colors and handsome "sets" make this quilt in Old Salem a real gem of its kind. No novice planned or pieced the curves that make up the large squares. It dates from about 1840 and shows the rather unusual color combinations of the area, as do the Drunkard's Path and T-Blocks in the same museum. The printed border is reminiscent of turn-of-the century quilts so that it has a transitional feeling of moving from styles of early nineteenth to mid-nineteenth century. One odd and interesting feature is the way that the quilting changes mid-block on the sides from a simple diamond to echoes of the crown. Look on p. 179 for diagrams.

T-BLOCKS   At a glance, you'd surely say that this quilt is modern, made to go with the strong clean lines of today's molded furniture. It is mid-19th century and comes from a Moravian family in Yadkin County, North Carolina. It is now in the Old Salem Restoration and was photographed there in the Vogler House. The design is not unusual; it is a nine patch called T-Blocks, closely related to Oddfellow's Cross and some of the Wild Geese designs. The color and dimensions are what give it the impact and up-to-date appearance. It is shown on a single bed in a boy's room because it is certainly the perfect quilt for a boy or young man. Diagrams and patterns are on pp. 180 & 181.

CAESAR'S CROWN *This entire design can be appliquéd on 16″ white squares, omitting piece no. 1. If you are fairly expert, you might want to piece the entire crown and then appliqué it onto the block, or you might want to lay out the pieces given here and create the correct shape for the large white corner piece, so that the entire square could be pieced. The latter option seems like more of a challenge than is necessary!*

The cross-bar "sets" are particularly effective in this quilt, but the squares can be set edge-to-edge (see Crown, p. 108) for a completely different appearance.

The quilting is done around the pieces and then as rather fine white work in the background areas. You might use either diagonals or echoing lines or a combination as was done on the original.

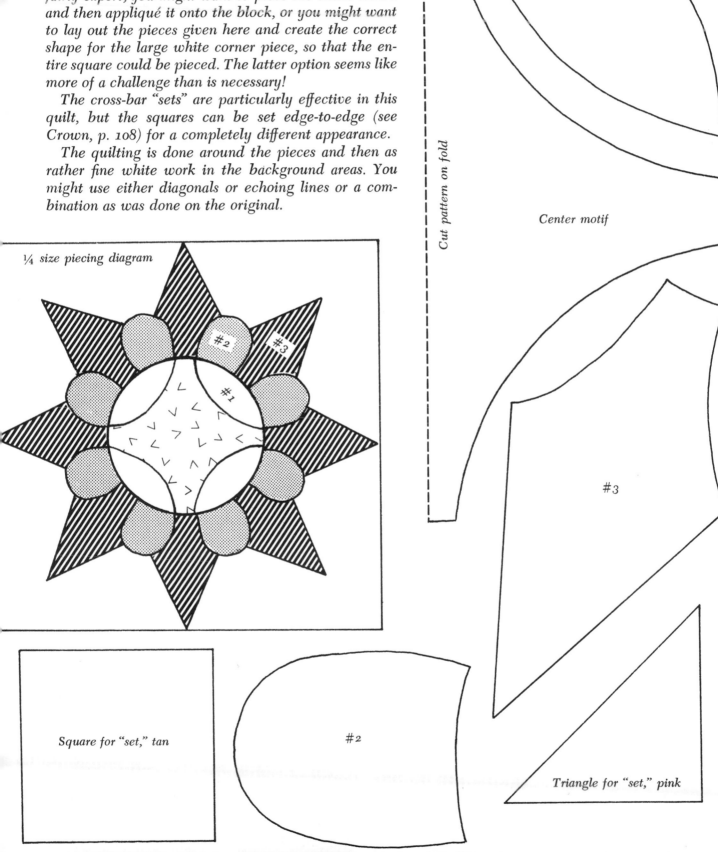

¼ size piecing diagram

Cut pattern on fold

#1

Center motif

#3

Square for "set," tan

#2

Triangle for "set," pink

Small triangle

T-BLOCKS   *The quilt is pieced, all straight line, suitable for beginners. Because of its large scale you might try it on the sewing machine if you really want to hurry it through.*

The cross-bar "sets" are cut 21″ x 3″ of a light orange shade. Three squares each way make a good single bed quilt with no border.

Most of the quilting is done around the blocks though there are a few other diagonal lines inside each block.

¼ *size piecing diagram*

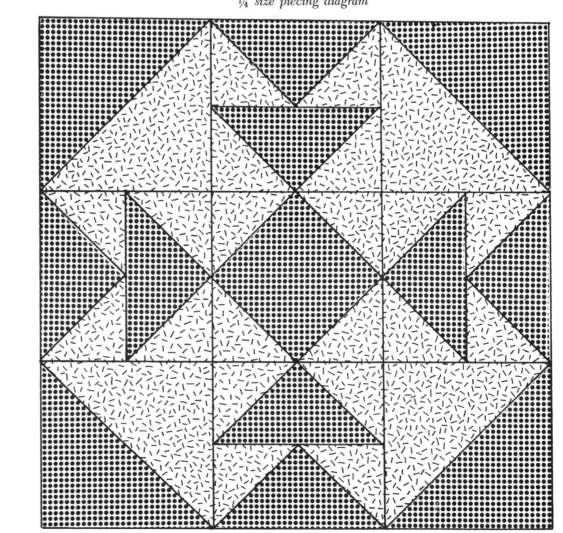

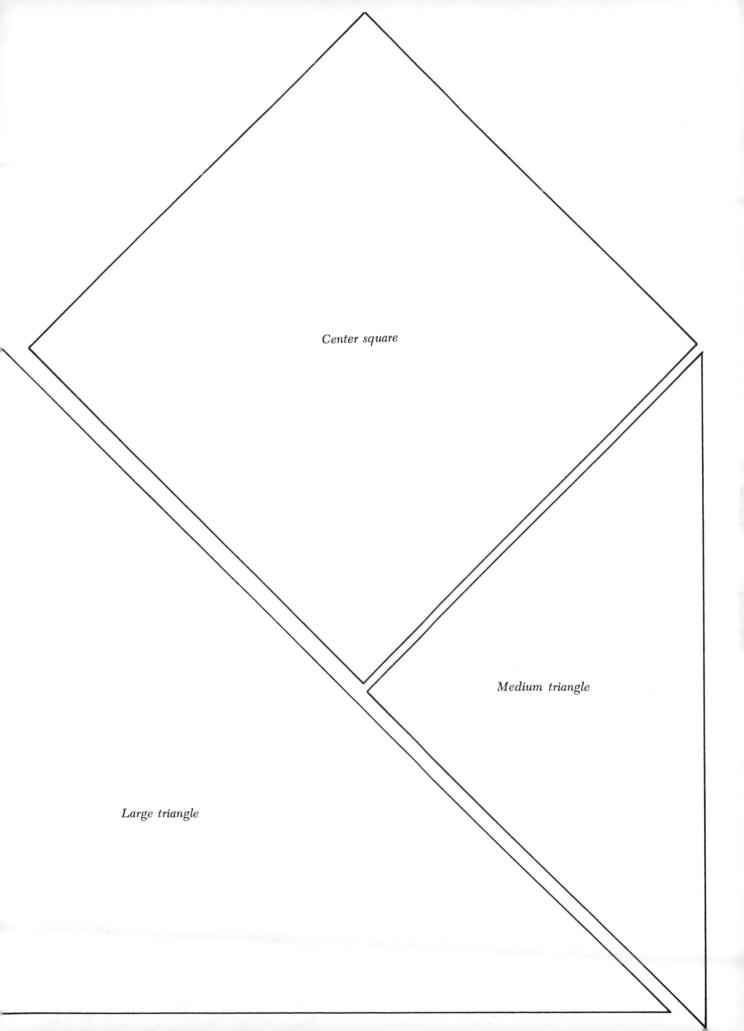

Center square

Medium triangle

Large triangle

PEARL S. BUCK BIRTHPLACE

West Virginia produced its share of heroes, many before it became a separate state, but it produced one extraordinary heroine in 1892, long after statehood. She was Pearl S. Buck, daughter of a missionary, Absolom Syndenstricker, and his wife Caroline, who were on home leave from their post in China. Her fame came after her first marriage so that she is known by her married name, Buck, to the millions who have read her books. In her last years and since her death the meaning of her name has continued to grow in the Pearl S. Buck Foundation which takes care of thousands of Amerasian children, mostly left by our soldiers in the Orient.

Though the house is a typical nineteenth century frame farmhouse, bright and well arranged, there are touches that tell interesting details of this remarkable family's life. In an upstairs bedroom, when Pearl Buck was born, there is a large cabinet with a design of Oriental dragons worked on the doors. There is also a music room which was a focal point for the family when they occupied the house on their home leaves. This shrine in Hillsboro is the first historical house to be opened to the public in West Virginia and worth stopping by, especially for the many who have enjoyed Pearl Buck's stories.

WEST VIRGINIA STAR   Stars made with diamond pieces can vary from the simple Lemon Star to the enormous Star of Bethlehem and in between there are a thousand variations according to the whim of the designer. The colors used, the way they are repeated, and the method of setting the stars together, all change the basic design in kaleidoscopic variations. We call this strong teal blue and dark brown version a West Virginia Star because it originated in the Beard family in Greenbriar County in that state. The probable date is just before the Civil War when this was a part of Virginia, but it is still in a private collection there and is shown in the music room in the Pearl Buck birthplace. For construction details see p. 183.

WEST VIRGINIA STAR   *Each star consists of eight points, pieced as shown. They are set together with 9" and 4½" white squares. The use of only two colors gives a depth to the design but it could be worked in scrapbag pieces if they were sorted carefully according to value.*

The borders are on the ends only and are 5" wide with appliquéd flower designs. The entire quilt is finished with white binding.

The only quilting is done around the star pieces and in a simple diagonal check in the white squares and border.

Full sized pattern and piecing diagram

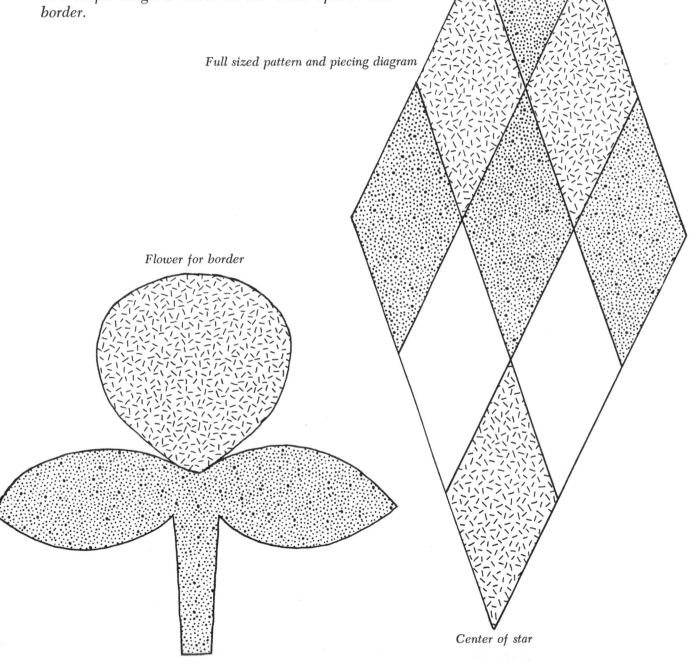

Flower for border

Center of star

MAJOR BUTLER GOODRICH HOUSE
(Part of Berkshire County Historical Society)

Pittsfield, Massachusetts, is fortunate in having rescued several of its 18th and 19th century buildings and put them under the protecting wing of a hard working historical society. The Goodrich House was built in 1793 and enlarged in 1813 as so many houses in that time of large families were. The Federal Period lines and spacious rooms give it a feeling of being built for all time. It is furnished with equally timeless excellent furniture, Queen Anne, Chippendale, Sheraton and Hepplewhite as well as some country pieces.

There are other buildings, including a remarkable 1871 School House in Stockbridge, which serve as museums and centers for educational and cultural activities. Throughout the year there are lectures and shows and craft demonstrations for the enjoyment of the local citizens as well as the people who summer in the Berkshires. The Berkshire Historical Society is the type of organization which more communities are forming all the time, and not a minute too soon!

CHECKERBOARD PATHS   Though closely related to Boston Commons and Country Lanes, this quilt seems to have been individually designed. It was made by Josephine Merrill of Berkshire County in 1868 for her brother, Charles E. Merrill, using a grand assortment of scrapbag pieces. Each piece is 1½″ inches square and, if you look carefully, you'll see that they are put together in large squares of 13½ inches and small ones of 4½ inches. The 1½ inch white squares and the 4½ inch white squares and 13½ by 4½ inch white rectangles are carefully arranged to give the interesting effect of continuous paths. The white work is also beautifully designed to create a curved effect around the large squares.

ROSE IN A WREATH   The same simple rose design that is used in so many variations is shown here in its most abstract form. It once belonged to Eliza Ann Smith (1842–1915) of Sheffield, Mass., and is now in the Berkshire Historical Society collection, where it is shown in the Goodrich House. It is in exceptionally good condition and the dark red and teal blue are brilliant and unfaded. Such a strong bold appliqué design would fit well in modern houses and could be made in many color variations or scrapbag pieces. Diagrams and patterns appear on p. 187.

ROSE IN A WREATH *Each square of this quilt is 11″ set with 1″ red bands. The teal blue rose and red wreath surrounded by teal leaves are appliquéd on a white background.*

The border is 9″ wide with eleven red padded grapes the size of a dime in each bunch. The vine is of ½″ wide bias of teal with teal leaves opposing each bunch of grapes.

The quilting outlines each part of the appliqué and forms a band of small scallops against the red set bands.

Full size pattern pieces as arranged in the squares

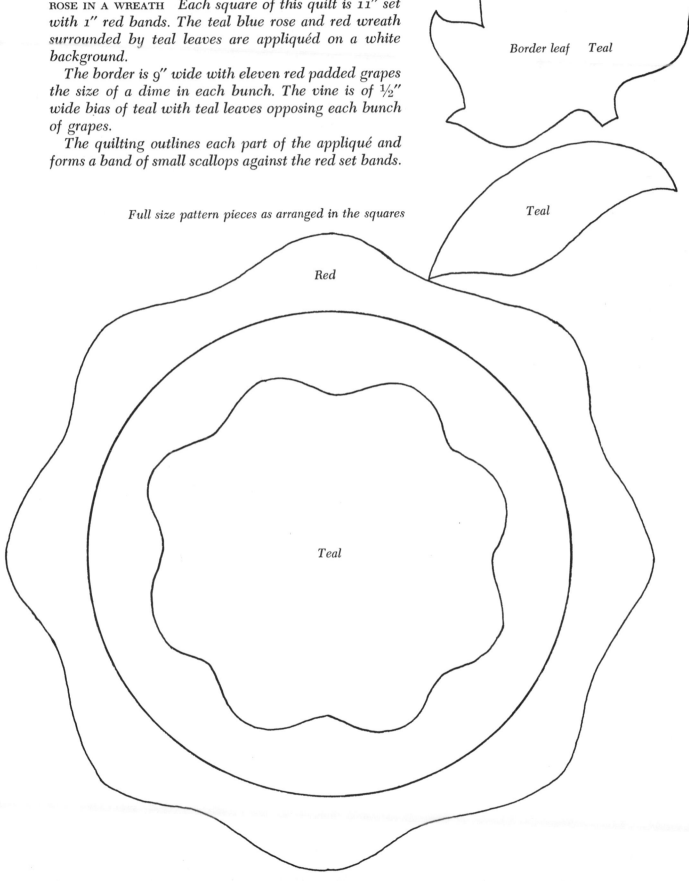

Border leaf   Teal

Teal

Red

Teal

MYSTIC MAZE Wonderful complicated looking optical illusion designs can be created like this one of strips of fabric arranged according to the designer's whim. The result here is of cool green latticed walks in a formal garden. It was pieced in the decade before 1850, but the same design could be appliquéd. It came from the family of Henry S. A. Black of Hancock, Mass. to the Berkshire Historical Society where it is shown in the Goodrich House. You will find a pattern diagram on p. 189 but this quilt may also serve as an interesting point of departure for ideas of your own.

MYSTIC MAZE   *The quilt is pieced, but could as well be appliquéd, of ⅞" green print strips on a white background. Three squares across and four in length make a nice double bed size with the addition of border and sets.*

The white inner bands or sets are 3" and the border 8". Each swag is approximately 9" long. The curved lines of the border help to create a less rigid effect.

The quilting is of the simplest diamond pattern.

½ size piecing diagram of one quarter of the square.   Center of square

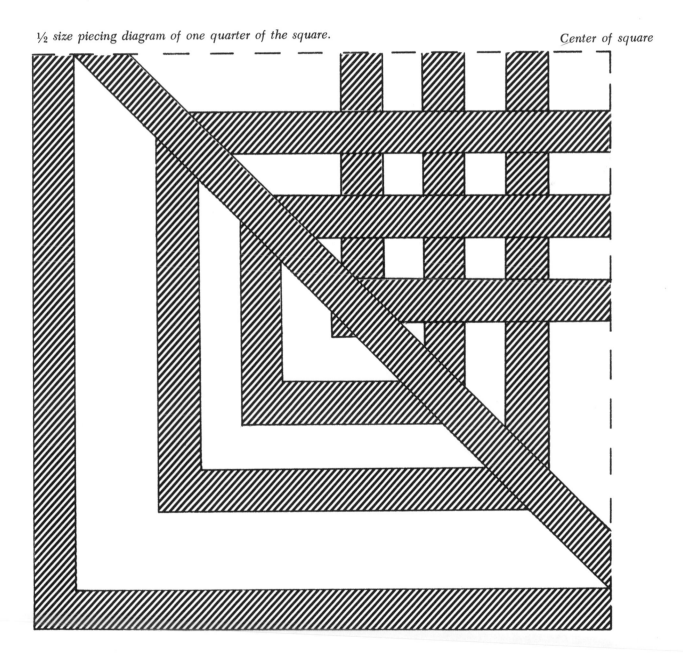

QUILTS IN PRIVATE COLLECTIONS

WHIG ROSE   A large elaborate Rose pattern developed in the hot political climate of the mid-nineteenth century. One hears such names as Democrat Rose and Whig Rose applied to a variety of designs made up of a stylized central rose and long rambling branches with buds, leaves and flowers. Whig Rose is the name which seems to have survived, though the political party suffered a different fate. This one, made by Rebecca Peck in Ballard, West Virginia, in 1851, is now in a private collection in that state. Actually, at the time it was made, Ballard was still in Virginia because West Virginia came into being during the Civil War, which may give a hint of exactly how hot the political climate was in those parts at that time. Patterns from which you can make your own variations, perhaps with a new political identificaton, are shown on pp. 191 & 192.

WHIG ROSE   *The center three sections of the large motif may be pieced together. They can then be appliquéd along with the other two pieces to the main squares. This will be most easily done if the no. 5 pieces are placed first, then the no. 4 and then the three center pieces, so that the scalloped pieces will overlap the plain pieces. Use ½″ bias for the stems and make any arrangement that you like of the buds, leaves and flowers. The quilt shown is made up of 27″ squares and 11″ borders, coming out to a very large 103″. For modern purposes, unless you're planning for a king-sized bed, it might be wise to cut down some on the size of the squares.*

The same stems, buds, leaves and flowers are used on the border. The long central vine on the border is a bias strip of about ⅞″.

The usual outline quilting is used around the motifs and some very fine and individual white work in the background.

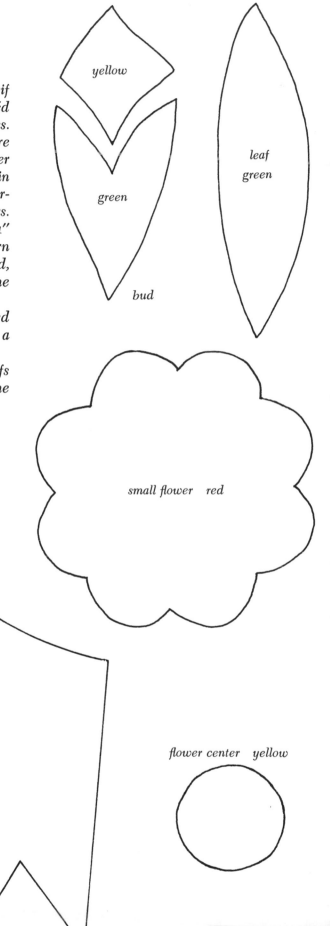

yellow

green

bud

leaf green

small flower   red

#5 green

flower center   yellow

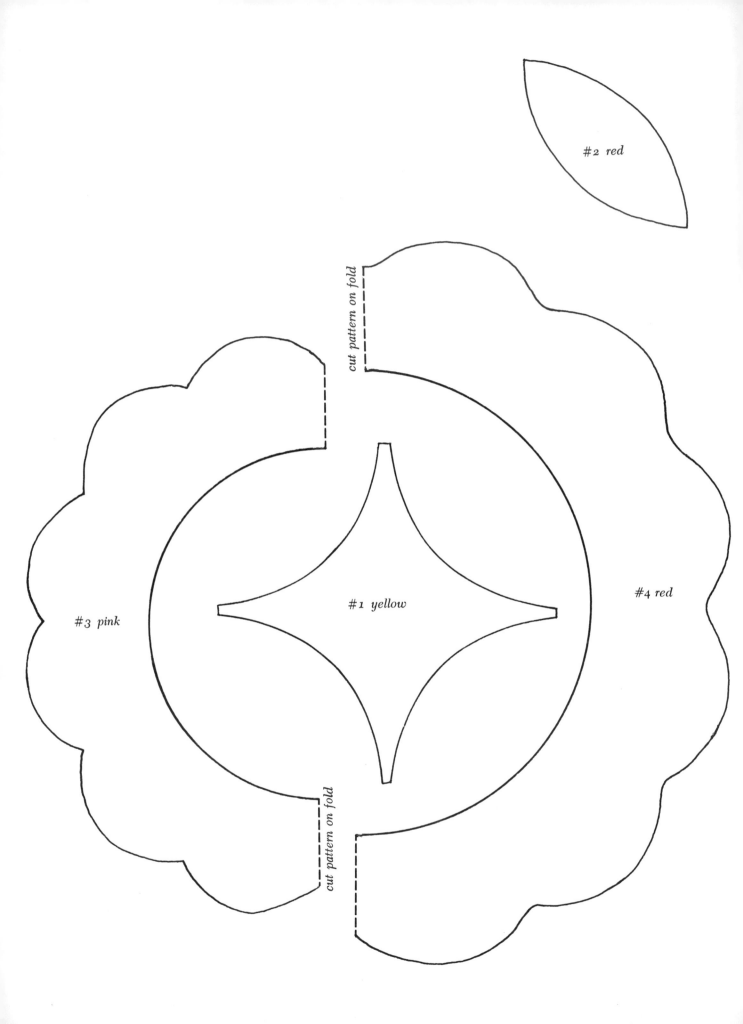

#2 red

cut pattern on fold

#3 pink

#1 yellow

#4 red

cut pattern on fold

NINE PATCH STRIPE Originality is the clue to so much interesting design but that doesn't have to mean something that is entirely new or shocking. This mid-nineteenth century quilt in a private collection in West Virginia is simplicity itself. The nine patch checkerboards are made from scrapbag pieces in an age-old style but the insertion of the heavily padded or Trapuntoed bands raises the whole to new heights. Each white work design is slightly different from all the others, but none would require any unusual artistic skill. This may even have been a way of using squares of an incompleted quilt which had been made and handed on to another quilter.

INDIVIDUAL INTERPRETATIONS   Wherever quilts were made in America the same motifs of Sunflowers and Sunbursts were used, but with what variations! These three from South Carolina, Kentucky and West Virginia are undoubtedly related but the final result and the feeling of each is so different. The simplest one, originally from South Carolina, but now in a private collection in North Carolina, has an almost childish naiveté in the style of its very fine needlework. It was made for M.A.C.V. by her mother in 1851, according to its signature.

The Kentucky one, highly padded and embellished, was made in Kentucky "before the colonies were states." The white work squares are varied, some having eagles, a favorite design, and others florals. The raised centers of the Sunflowers and the surrounding buds are stuffed so tightly that it is amazing they have not burst. The quilting is fine enough that there is no doubt as to this being a Masterpiece Quilt. It is now in a private collection in West Virginia.

The last of these Sunburst designs was started in the nineteenth century by Caroline Sydenstricker in her home in West Virginia, which is now a memorial to her daughter, Pearl Buck. The quilt was finished later and is shown in the room where Pearl Buck was born while her family was on leave from their missionary duties in China. The colors are bold and the background red, which makes a complete change from the other two.

There are many subtle differences between these designs as well as the obvious ones. If you look at the quilting design used with the Feathered Star, p. 175, you will see this design in its purest form, with sixteen points or petals, drawn so as to form two more groups of an equal number of sections. The Mariner's Compass on p. 159 also bears a family resemblance, again planned with mathematical precision. The Sunflowers shown here seem somewhat random by comparison, the first having seven petals, the next thirteen and the last fourteen. Each in its way has a charm totally unrelated to the perfection of the planning and patterning, which should give twentieth century quilters the courage to launch out and make their quilts as they see them, not as copies of someone else's nineteenth century plans.

A highly padded design from Kentucky, now in a private collection in W. Virginia.

(Top) Sunburst made in S. Carolina, now in a private collection in N. Carolina.

(Bottom) Pearl Buck quilt, now in her restored birthplace in W. Virginia.

SUPPLIERS OF QUILTING EQUIPMENT

For cotton fabrics:

Vermont Country Store
Weston, Vt. 05161
    (send 75¢ for samples)

Quilts and Other Comforts
P.O. Box 394
Wheatridge, Col. 80033
    (small charge for samples)

For cotton quilting thread, white and colors:

Quilts and Other Comforts
P.O. Box 394
Wheatridge, Col. 80033

For Mountain Mist batting and stuffing:

Creative Quilting Center
The Stearns & Foster Co.
11750 Chesterdale Rd.
Cincinnati, Ohio 45246

For patterns and templates:

Contemporary Quilts
5305 Denwood Ave.
Memphis, Tenn. 38117
    (will make custom designs)

Quilts and Other Comforts
P.O. Box 394
Wheatridge, Col. 80033

Creative Quilting Center
The Stearns & Foster Co.
11750 Chesterdale Rd.
Cincinnati, Ohio 45246

For a blue print of the standing frame:

Creative Quilting Center
The Stearns & Foster Co.
11750 Chesterdale Rd.
Cincinnati, Ohio 45246
    (small charge for handling and mailing)

For current and continuing quilt information, subscribe to:

Quilter's Newsletter
P.O. Box 394
Wheatridge, Col. 80033

Lady's Circle Patchwork Quilts
23 West 26th St.
New York, N.Y. 10010

INDEX OF QUILTS AND PATTERNS

INDEX OF PLACES WHERE QUILTS MAY BE SEEN